Franz Schubert

1797-1828

Fryderyk Chopin

1810-1849

Franz Liszt

1811-1886

Staff Credits

Editors
David Buxton BA (Honours)
Sue Lyon BA (Honours)

Art Editors
Debbie Jecock BA (Honours)
Ray Leaning BA (Honours),
PGCE (Art & Design)

Deputy Editor
Barbara Segall BA

Sub-editors
Geraldine Jones
Judy Oliver BA (Honours)
Nigel Rodgers BA (Honours), MA
Penny Smith
Will Steeds BA (Honours), MA

Designers
Steve Chilcott BA (Honours)
Shirin Patel BA (Honours)
Chris Rathbone

Picture Researchers
Georgina Barker
Julia Calloway BA (Honours)
Vanessa Cawley

Production Controllers
Sue Fuller
Steve Roberts

Secretary
Lynn Smail

Publisher
Terry Waters Grad IOP

Editorial Director
Maggi McCormick

Production Executive
Robert Paulley BSc

Managing Editor
Alan Ross BA (Honours)

Consultants
Dr Antony Hopkins
Commander of the Order
of the British Empire,
Fellow of the
Royal College of Music

Nick Mapstone BA (Honours), MA

Keith Shadwick BA (Honours)

Reference Edition Published 1990

Published by Marshall Cavendish Corporation
147 West Merrick Road
Freeport, Long Island
N.Y. 11520

Typeset by Walkergate Press Ltd, Hull, England
Printed and bound in Singapore by
Times Offset Private Ltd.

Library of Congress Cataloging-in-Publication Data

The Great composers, their lives and times.
Includes index.
1. Composers—Biography. 2. Music appreciation.
I. Marshall Cavendish Corporation.
ML390.G82 1987 780'.92'2 [B] 86-31294
ISBN 0-86307-776-5

ISBN 0-86307-776-5 (set)
0-86307-782-X (vol)

Franz Schubert

1797-1828

Fryderyk Chopin

1810-1849

Franz Liszt

1811-1886

MARSHALL CAVENDISH
NEW YORK · LONDON · SYDNEY

Contents

Introduction

Webster's Dictionary ***defines 'romantic' as meaning 'without a basis in fact; fanciful, fictitious', but in the late-18th and early-19th centuries, Romanticism was a movement of intellectual thought in reaction to what contemporary artists believed to be the worship of reason by the Classical era. Although the Romantics found much to admire in Mozart's works, especially his operas, they rejected what they saw as the cold reasonableness of composers like Haydn. In place of order, the Romantics exalted emotions, beauty and instinct; while most of the older generation recoiled from the French Revolution, young poets like Wordsworth, Shelley and Keats welcomed 1789 as the dawn of a new age in which the human spirit would be freed; whereas the Age of Reason distrusted Nature unless it was tamed in landscaped parkland, Romanticism loved the natural world for its wildness and unpredictability and found artistic and spiritual inspiration in Nature's untamed beauty.***

Of course, Romanticism did not replace Classicism overnight, and in composers of the Romantic age such as Schubert and Chopin elements of the Classical can be discerned. Their music has a purity and lack of flamboyance that is distinctly un-Romantic, though in their short, tragic lives, dogged by illness, they provided archetypes for the struggling, doomed Romantic artist. Franz Liszt, with his virtuoso playing and charismatic physical presence, was a true Romantic hero. But like Schubert and Chopin, he was a composer of true originality and his music expresses the Romantic style in its highest form.

THE GREAT COMPOSERS

Franz Schubert

1797-1828

Franz Peter Schubert was one of the greatest composers of the early 19th century. Franz Liszt called him 'the greatest ever poet', and Schubert's poetic vision did indeed breathe new life into old forms. His music is composed in the formal styles of the Classical age, but is Romantic in its poetry, subjective vision and revolutionary language. Schubert therefore stands at the beginning and end of two eras of music, and belongs as much to the age of Mozart and Beethoven as to that of Chopin and Liszt. The clarity and directness of Schubert's music have made him a favourite with professional musicians and public alike, and the following pages examine the qualities that make him such a great and popular composer. His contribution to the development of song is assessed, while the Listener's Guide, *analyzes some of his best-known works. Finally,* In the Background *looks at contemporary fashion and the city of Vienna, where Schubert was born and lived all his life.*

COMPOSER'S LIFE

'Schwammerl'

Short, chubby and bespectacled, Schubert may have lacked glamour, but his musical talents were much respected and his warm, friendly nature made him loved by all who knew him.

Schubert (above) transcended the trials of his often unhappy life to compose ethereal, sparkling music that in its wit, charm and range of feeling, truly reflected the humanity of his genius.

Many composers of the Classical and Romantic eras wrote intensely personal music, but few wrote music so endearingly human as Franz Peter Schubert. Mozart's music is magical but gives little impression of the man; Haydn's shows a craftsman at work. Yet with Schubert it is as if we were standing at his shoulder, watching him at work and sharing his innermost thoughts as a composer.

The first thing we learn about Schubert from the writings and letters of his friends and acquaintances is, as we would hope from knowing him only through his music, that he was greatly loved, though by no means uncritically, by those who knew him. All his friends were fiercely loyal, although sometimes he did not realize it. The playwright Eduard von Bauernfeld, a close friend, remembered him as 'the most honest soul and the most faithful friend' and later, in an obituary poem, wrote:

So true and honest, not of common clay,
So free from artifice, so skilled in art.
A single mind his guide through all the days,
Which made him thoughtful, yet did joy impart.

The writer also tells us, however, that he was 'more taciturn than other mortals'. It seems that Schubert had a warm, friendly nature that had to be discovered behind a natural shyness and reticence. His artist friend Moritz von Schwind remarked in retrospect: 'The more I realize now what he was like, the more I

Archiv für Kunst und Geschichte

Franz Theodor Schubert, (left), the composer's father, loved music and always encouraged his son's musical talent. They would often have musical evenings together when young Franz would gently correct Papa's mistakes.

see what he has suffered'. From these and oth comments we begin to get a picture of a man who w dominated, sometimes unwillingly, by the force of h genius and yet desperately unable to make the best us of his gifts – at least in a worldly sense. The warmth his nature is reflected in his music but the shyness th came partly from his humble origins made him to timid to challenge the musical establishment, so th throughout his life Schubert saw much lesser me than himself gaining all the honours.

His friends found him very stubborn at times. H would fall out with those who could and would hav helped him, squandering many chances that were p his way. This partly accounted for his lack of success i the competitive world of the theatre. Lack of effort hardly a fault to pin on one who wrote so much in comparatively short life, yet unfinished works ar frequent and several have movements half sketche but never completed.

Very little is known about his working hours, f these he spent very much alone. In the evenings, in th coffee houses and taverns, he became cheerful an outgoing. But there is little doubt that he was of depressive nature rarely able to escape from hi reclusive tendencies without the help of alcohol. An

The Imperial and Royal School in Vienna (right), where young Schubert was a choirboy and pupil for five years from 1808 until 1813. By the time he started at the school at the age of 11, he was already a prolific composer and a talented pianist and violinist. Teachers found there was little they could teach him about music.

Historisches Museum, Vienna

Pages from Schubert's diary (left) for 13th June, 1816, a day made unforgettable for him by a performance of a Mozart quintet. 'A light and bright, beautiful day,' Schubert writes, 'I shall remember it throughout my whole life – I still hear as if from afar, the magic sound of Mozart's music . . . Oh! Mozart! Immortal Mozart, how many visions of a brighter and better world you have imprinted on our souls!' They were indeed firmly imprinted on Schubert's soul, and Mozart's influence can be heard in many of his works.

hile at the Imperial nd Royal School, chubert made a great npression on the minent composer ntonio Salieri (above) ho gave him lessons in omposition.

then he would over-indulge his liking for good wine, which he refused to dilute with water, as was the Viennese custom, often becoming boisterous and even violent and, in the final stages, morose and brooding. Schwind believed that Schubert did much to damage his health by his heavy drinking and thus hastened his early death. There were many embarrassing scenes before his friends helped him back to his room in the small hours of the morning. Having slept it off, he would work in solitude all the next day and then emerge again for yet another riotous evening.

Physically, Schubert had little on his side. He was very short in stature, standing about five-feet-one, and plumply built so that his friends gave him the nickname of *Schwammerl* – 'the little mushroom', or, to put it into English schoolboy terms 'Tubby'. He had a round, fat face, short neck and not too high a forehead. Those searching for some redeeming features in their description mention well-shaped (though thickish) lips and a dimpled chin. According to his friend Sonnleithner he had 'a mass of brown and naturally curly hair, round shoulders and back, chubby arms and hands with short fingers – and, if I remember rightly, grey-blue eyes'. He walked in a hunched-up sort of way and his expression was 'generally obtuse and inclined to be sullen'. However, everyone seems to agree that when he was interested in a conversation or listening to music his face became alive and he had a sweet-natured smile.

We have the benefit of several portraits of Schubert painted by friends during his lifetime and, though they do not entirely agree and some cannot resist the obvious temptation to romanticize, there is no getting away from the short stumpy nose and the short-sighted eyes (his sight was bad from boyhood) behind the ill-fitting spectacles which are still kept in the Schubert museum in Vienna. In later years when Moritz von Schwind was asked to sum up his appearance he described him as 'a drunken cabby'. Others have added their mite of deprecation by describing him as 'a Bavarian peasant' and 'undistinguished'.

In the end, of course, these things matter very little. They all loved their small, shy, gentle friend; and posterity does not demand that those who write like angels should necessarily look like them.

Early years in Vienna

It is strange that of all the great composers whom we think of as Viennese through their association with the city, Mozart and Beethoven among them, only Schubert was actually born there. He was the son of a poverty-stricken teacher who ran a private school in a Viennese suburb, and an erstwhile cook. Living in inadequate conditions and rarely well-fed, his parents had attempted to raise no less than 11 children before Franz Peter came on the scene. Of these only the first, Ignaz, and the last two, Ferdinand and Franz Karl survived into adulthood.

Franz Peter Schubert was born on 31 January 1797, in a small room used as a kitchen, and was duly baptized as a Catholic. Little is known of his early childhood but we imagine a stocky but unathletic child, short-sighted and intellectually inclined, who studied at his father's school from around 1803. Father Franz did all he could to interest his children in music, and the elder brother Ignaz, by then about 17 and teaching at the school, attempted to nurture Schubert's obvious early talents. He soon admitted that his pupil had natural abilities that went far beyond his own and that he could teach him nothing. Schubert began writing compositions for the family and by the age of ten he was the leading singer in the local church

Archiv für Kunst und Geschichte

Despite his quietness, Schubert's presence was much valued on social occasions and it is not surprising to see pictures of him on a picnic – an open-air 'Schubertiad' – with his friends (right).

Mary Evans Picture Library

Many evenings found Schubert sitting in the cafés of Vienna like the one above, drinking wine (not diluted with water unlike the Viennese custom) until he staggered home late at night.

choir and was writing music to be performed there.

In 1808, he was admitted to the Court Chapel choir at the Imperial and Royal School. If there was some initial excitement at the donning of the military-styled uniform there was also the sudden realization of the rather bleak regime that such a life entailed. It was very much a round of hard work with school lessons all day, music lessons in the evening and very few weekends when there was not some concert or service; and visits from his family were rare. There were many typical schoolboy notes from Schubert asking for a little more pocket-money and some food to enhance a meagre diet: 'After a so-so lunch we've to wait eight and a half hours for a rotten supper'.

He did reasonably well at his general studies and, of course, found the musical studies no trouble at all. 'A very special musical talent' said his report at the end of the second term. The grounding and opportunities were unsurpassable. As well as singing in the choir, Schubert played in the school orchestra and became familiar with the music of composers such as Haydn and Mozart with occasional sorties into the work of the 'moderns' like Beethoven. Fellow pupils remembered Schubert as 'shy and uncommunicative' and he would spend most of his spare time composing and practising in a deserted room.

In truth, Schubert's father had some doubts about the wisdom of a musical career and would have preferred his son to follow his own calling as a teacher. Schubert's mother died in May 1812 and at this time father and son were drawn much closer together. When Schubert's voice broke in July he had to leave the choir, but his father agreed that he could stay at the school for another year if he would work hard at his academic studies as well as the music. It was to be a fruitful year. Schubert was taken on by Kapellmeister Antonio Salieri as his special pupil in harmony and counterpoint and they got on well. Schubert was

Schubert fell in love wit Therese Grob (above) and would have married her had he no been so poor – her parents insisted she married a wealthy baker.

Archiv für Kunst und Geschichte

Schubert's friends were very important to him, not only for company, but because they did everything they could to promote his music. He is pictured above with his two associates, Anselm Hüttenbrenner and Johann Jenger.

lways proud to call himself 'a pupil of Salieri'; while ne master, like everyone else, simply proclaimed that e found that Schubert 'knew everything there was to now about music' without much help from him.

reluctant schoolmaster

t this time Schubert was offered a scholarship by the mperor but, as music was given least priority in the ourse of studies offered, he declined it and decided to umour his father by joining the family school as a nior master. There was much family rejoicing, but chubert loathed the work. It was not at all easy for a erson of his nature and was very poorly paid. His ather had remarried and Franz got on well with his epmother who helped him with money. He stayed at ne school until 1816 and, in spite of its demands, his nree years as a teacher proved to be fruitful ones. During this time he wrote around 400 compositions ncluding his first three symphonies, some of his early ttempts at opera, string quartets, masses and some 50 songs in which he gradually found his true style. He had his first considerable success with a song *Gretchen am Spinnrade* ('Gretchen at the spinning-wheel'), a setting of words by Goethe which was passed around among his friends and sung at many mateur concerts.

Schubert was at this time making the acquaintance f a brilliant young pianist Mme Jenny and his houghts at this time were occasionally directed oward the fairer sex. He fell in love with Therese Grob, the young daughter of a friend of the family who ad sung in his Mass in F at the local church. The affair ontinued for a while but as an impoverished choolmaster he was in no position to marry and ventually she wed a wealthy baker.

By early 1816 he had grown thoroughly tired of oping with unwilling pupils and decided to gain his reedom. He wrote for the vacant post of Music Director in Laibach, citing Salieri as his reference. However, Salieri was not entirely to be trusted. He recommended another pupil and Schubert was turned down. Throughout his life he was to find similar difficulty in obtaining official support and it made him ever more reluctant to seek it. However, Schubert buried his resentment and wrote a cantata to celebrate Salieri's 66th birthday.

In his diaries he ruefully remarks that 'Man is the plaything of chance and passion – to some it is given and others have to struggle.' With the fair Therese in mind he finds 'the idea of marriage full of terror for the single man'. He continued to take his daily walks in the country and refresh his mind with its beauties. And he proudly notes, on 17 June 1816: 'I composed today for the first time for money. Namely a cantata for Professor Watteroth's name day to words by Dräxler. The fee is 100 Viennese florins'.

The young composer

So Schubert stepped out into the world to become a composer. Leaving home he lodged for a while with his friend Josef Spaun. Through him he now met a another medical student, Franz von Schober, whose rich Viennese family were keen patrons of the arts and lived an unconventionally Bohemian life. In the autumn, Schober persuaded Schubert to move into the family home and tried to help him in every way. It was there that he met the famous singer Michael Vogl (whom he had heard singing Gluck) and diffidently showed him one of his songs. Vogl declared it was not bad but secretly he was greatly impressed and soon became a great champion of Schubert's music. His performances of the songs did a great deal to get Schubert known in Vienna.

By 1817 he had written some of his most attractive songs such as *Die Forelle* ('The Trout') and *An die Musik* ('To Music'), so essentially Schubertian in their melodic grace and flow, as well as dramatic pieces like *Der Tod und das Mädchen* ('Death and the maiden'). He worked on his 4th Symphony which had a definite flavour and style of Beethoven about it, and composed the carefree 5th Symphony, which is infused with the spirit of Mozart. Although his music was still considered daring and unconventional he was gradually being taken up by the fashionable 'Biedermeier' society of the day; the drawing-room society people who lived their cultural and intellectual lives in a careful avoidance of the controversial political and revolutionary stirrings of the times.

In fact, Schubert himself often grew tired of the endless socializing and he was glad to be offered employment for the summer of 1818 as a music tutor to the two young daughters of Count Esterházy a hundred miles from Vienna in Zseliz. It was his first long journey outside Vienna and he enjoyed the leisurely life as well as a mild flirtation with a pretty lady's maid called Pepi. But even this began to pall and he was glad to return to Vienna for the winter. Through influential friends he now got his first commission for a one-act opera for which he was paid some 50 pounds.

In the summer of 1819 he went for a trip into the Austrian countryside with Michael Vogl as his companion. It was one of the happiest periods of his life and, while staying with an old friend Albert Stadler he wrote a sparkling piano quintet for the local musical society with a variation movement based on his *Die Forelle* – the happily inspired 'Trout' quintet. Back in Vienna for the winter of 1819–20 he was almost involved in an unpleasant brush with the authorities. He was at a party when his friend Johann Senn was arrested (he later spent a year in prison); the inoffensive Schubert was allowed to go free.

By 1821 he was becoming reasonably well-known as a composer and was given a job at the Court Theatre. But his unpunctuality and lack of cooperation soon put an end to this. His income came mainly from the modest fees that he could command for his drawing-room appearances. At these he would perform his duties well enough but refused to socialize and hated the praises and speeches at the end. He was happy enough being left to improvise at the piano while the young people danced. But his work was still not published and some of his friends thought it high time that it was. Sonnleithner, Josef Hüttenbrenner and others got together and persuaded the publisher Diabelli to put out some of Schubert's best songs on a sale or return basis. The first was *Erlkönig* in April 1821 and others quickly followed. It brought him a small but regular income from his music at last.

A rather fanciful picture of Schubert at the piano (above) painted by Gustav Klimt around 1900 but it creates a wonderful impression of the gentle gaiety of Schubert's music.

Illness and despair

In 1822, probably after one of the customary drunken evenings, Schubert was persuaded by some of his drinking friends to visit a brothel. It was typical of his luck that he was the only one to suffer from this, contracting a serious dose of syphilis which was to have tragic consequences. The disease and the ensuing painful mercury treatment made him desperately ill and he spent the early part of 1823 in hospital. It weakened an already unstable constitution and he was a long while recovering. It was at this time that he wrote: 'There is no man in the world as wretched and unhappy as I'; it was a bleak time after what had seemed a hopeful period. His 'Unfinished' Symphony, written at the end of 1822, seems to be born from the depths of personal tragedy.

By this time even the happy world of the Schubertiads (as the evenings with his friends were known) was beginning to disintegrate. From now on it was a life that alternated between occasional hope and happiness and deep depression., His friends scattered (even his great ally Vogl was now in retirement). He kept in touch sporadically, writing to Kupelwieser the painter in 1824:

Imagine someone whose health will never be right again, and whose sheer despair makes things ever worse rather than trying to improve matters; imagine someone whose highest hopes have been dashed and to whom the happiness of love and friendship brings only pain; whose enthusiasm for all things beautiful threatens to forsake him – and I ask you if such a one is not a wretched and unhappy being? Each evening when I retire to bed I hope I may not wake again; and each morning brings back yesterday's grief.

Yet despite his doubtful health and moods of gloom and despondency, his friends would often find him busy and wrapped in his work, turning out the sunny Octet and, in the summer of 1825, probably writing the great and glorious C major Symphony. Even the origins of this are clouded in surmise. That summer of 1825 he went to Hungary with Vogl and repeated some of the pleasures they had experienced on their first trip together. In 1826 his friends again made various efforts to get him an official post but all of these failed.

A tragic end

In the darkest of moods Schubert sat down and wrote his song-cycle *Winterreise* ('Winter Journey'). He warned his friends that they would be shaken by it; and they were. The bitterness and sense of despair in the songs made even the optimistic Schober feel gloomy. Yet, in all his grief, Schubert was still to write some of his most beautiful and often profound music – the two glorious Piano Trios and the great String Quintet included; and various offers from publishers induced a small degree of optimism again. He revised the score of the C Major Symphony for the *Musikverein* but they found it too difficult to play and it was not performed until 1839. There was a very special pleasure for him in a concert of his music on 26 March, 1828 when the E flat Piano Trio was played. Yet even this was marred by public attention being turned to the magical violin playing of the great Paganini who had given his first concert in Vienna just before. The papers were so full of the Italian 'comet' that there was no room for any mention of Schubert's music.

That year, Schubert had been studying Handel's music and decided to arrange lessons in counterpoint. 'Now for the first time I see what I lack.' But before he could start the lessons, he fell seriously ill again and moved into his brother Ferdinand's house so that he could have the comfort of a little attention. In October, 1828, he went for a short holiday to Eisenstadt where he brooded long over the grave of Haydn. Returning to Vienna his sickness grew worse but he managed to take walks and to work a little until 11 November, when he took to his bed. He tried hard to regain his strength, but on the 16th he suddenly deteriorated and a nervous fever was diagnosed. On the afternoon of the 19th, with Ferdinand and the doctor at his side, Schubert suddenly grasped at the wall and, murmuring 'This is my end', he died.

Attended by heart-broken friends and family his body was taken to the cemetery at Wahring and buried in a grave next to Beethoven's. On his tombstone an epitaph by Grillparzer, a contemporary poet, was engraved: 'The art of music here entombed a fair possession, but even fairer hopes'.

Vienna pays tribute to Schubert, one of its greatest sons, in this statue in the Stadtpark (right). But the grim, imposing statue seems far removed from the human, gentle 'Schwammerl'.

Bildarchiv Preussischer Kulturbesitz

COMPOSER'S LIFE

Schubert and song

Schubert was an immense influence on the development of song, not only because of his vast output – he wrote over 600 songs during his short life – but also because he was the first great composer to make the music complementary to the lyrics (words) of the song, rather than merely an accompaniment to them. His two greatest song-cycles (sequences of songs with a linking theme) are Die schöne Müllerin *(The Fair Maid of the Mill) and* Winterreise *(Winter Journey). The former was written when the future still seemed to promise much, but* Winterreise *reflects Schubert's own despair and disappointment at the end of his life. Whatever their atmosphere, Schubert's songs were originally performed in the* Schubertadien *concert parties held in the homes of his friends and patrons, and, although they are now performed in the formal setting of a concert hall, his songs still have a direct, simple and enduring appeal to his audiences.*

COMPOSER'S LIFE

'So true and honest'

Through a veritable treasury of songs, Schubert responded with imaginative genius to the poetry that he loved. In doing so, this many-sided composer set a new standard for a neglected musical form.

Julius Schmid 'Ein Schubert-Abend in einem Wiener Bürgerhaus'. Museen der Stadt Wien/The Bridgeman Art Library

chubert's songs found sympathetic and ppreciative audience i his friends at their egular evening soirées, nown affectionately as* chubertiaden *(above). hen, as now, their eautiful, highly ingable' melodies had direct and enduring ppeal.

Die Forelle (The Trout), the gem embedded in the famous 'Trout' Quintet, was among the earliest of Schubert's songs to become well known through private circulation in and around Vienna. It clearly represents the lighter side of his nature; a part of him that was in constant rivalry with his deeper, more pessimistic inclinations. The greatness of Schubert is revealed in his finest works when the two strands combine to create works that are both eminently approachable and deeply moving. Schubert's achievement as a songwriter was immense (he wrote just over 600 songs in his tragically short life) and it is in his songs that this creative struggle can be most clearly seen.

A song like *Die Forelle,* basically of the folk-song variety with several repeated verses, has an ancestry so long that it is untraceable. Even in the development of the more contrived sort of song (the art-song as it is rather off-puttingly known), Schubert is well down the family tree and had the example of many masters of song before him. Almost all music was once folk-music, all song was once folk-song, and every composer who identifies himself with his country, as most do, must consciously or unconsciously borrow folk-tunes and copy the style. A spontaneous composer such as Schubert would, in earlier times, have been an anonymous purveyor of folk-music, as would Mozart and many others.

In these days, when music has become a great commerce, the 'serious' composer has more or less cut himself off from the world of popular music, which is written by people no less specialized in their craft. Up to the time of Mozart and Schubert and a little later, the composer was in a less clearly defined position and both Mozart and Schubert devoted much of their time to providing popular music (of a high-class kind but nevertheless suited to lower and middle-brow tastes) in song and dance form.

Composers, however, were gradually beginning the process of specialization, confining themselves to writing music and drawing upon the services of the professional poet for the words. In the musical periods up to the 18th century it is loosely true to say that the composers were concerned to a lesser degree than in the 19th century with securely matching words to music which underlined their meaning and did nothing to detract from it. It was then more a case of matching verbal felicities with musical ones.

Schubert, right on the threshold of the Romantic era, could still write songs in which the music did not restrain its natural melodic spirit in order to underline the meaning – *Die Forelle* is an example – indeed, he often chose rather minor and insignificant poetry which his music enhanced. It is not often that very great poetry is found suitable for setting to music except where its greatness lies in a lyrical force such as

Schubert began by modelling his songs on those of minor composers such as Zumsteeg, Zelter (Mendelssohn's teacher) and Reichardt (right). He soon far surpassed his models in his sensitivity to the poetry of the verse he set and in his spontaneous gift for melody.

It is often claimed that the history of the 'art-song' begins with Schubert. However, song had been a high art-form since the days of the minstrel (below). Schubert, though, differed from his forbears, in that he made the music complementary to the words, rather than merely an accompaniment.

Anton Kraus 'Minnesänger mit seinem Knappen' München, Schackgalerie. Joachim Blauel/Artothek

J.H.W. Tischbein 'Goethe in der römischen Campagna' Frankfurt, Städelsches Kunstinstitut. Joachim Blauel/Artothek

Johann Michael Vogl (left), the famous baritone, became one of Schubert's warmest admirers and an invaluable interpreter of his songs.

Goethe (below), the great philosopher and Germany's finest lyric poet, inspired some of Schubert's most perfect songs. It seems that the young composer was struck by the force and clarity of Goethe's lines – qualities that find a clear parallel in his music. Josef von Spaun sent Goethe a volume of Schubert's settings of his poems, with a request that they might dedicate it to the poet. But the songs were returned without comment.

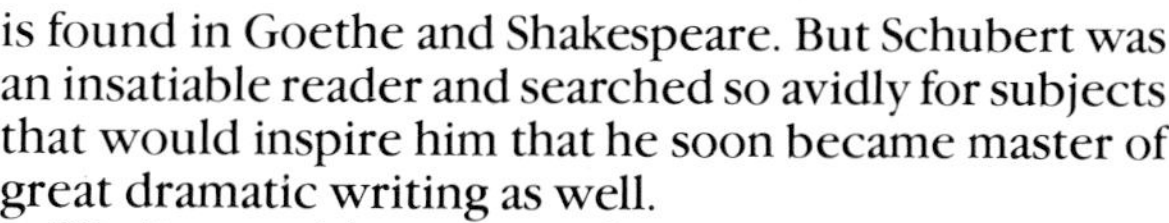

is found in Goethe and Shakespeare. But Schubert was an insatiable reader and searched so avidly for subjects that would inspire him that he soon became master of great dramatic writing as well.

His literary ideas were often given life by his great love of nature. In his diary for 14 June, 1816 he wrote:

I took an evening walk for once, as I had not done for several months. There can be scarcely anything more agreeable than to enjoy the green country on an evening after a hot summer's day, a pleasure for which the fields between Währing and Döbling seem to have been especially created. In the uncertain twilight and in the company of my brother Karl, my heart warmed within me.

Richard Capell in his classic study *Schubert's Songs* affirms this viewpoint:

The first glance at Schubert suggests a rippling movement . . . the variety and unsurprising naturalness of moving water and springing herb. There is no avoiding the thought of nature in connexion with Schubert.

Poetic inspiration

Much of the power that literary thought began to exert on 19th-century composers such as Schubert surely stems from the greatness of Shakespeare. Firstly, in the direct influence of his lyrics which are so instinctively musical – and were probably, in many cases, written with folk-tunes in mind – that they hardly need a musical setting at all. They are the natural link. At second-hand, the spirit of Shakespeare haunted and influenced the poets who followed, particularly in England and Germany. He was one of the supreme sources of the Romantic spirit.

Schubert lived in an age when German poetry was at one of its great peaks. And poetry meant more to him than possibly it had meant to any earlier composer. As if to emphasize this, nearly all of his friends were writers and poets, and those who were not were painters. He rarely kept company with fellow composers and few of his friends were musicians. He clearly had a firm idea of what he wanted to find in poetry. Over 70 of his songs were settings of music by the great Goethe, the supreme genius among them. Some ideal material he missed altogether and he only came upon Heine toward the end of his life. Often he would search the minor poets, of which there were plenty, alight on the one piece he wanted and, as in the case of Christian Schubart, immortalize someone who would otherwise have been forgotten by an inspired setting such as *Die Forelle.*

After Goethe, Schubert found a rich source of poetry in the works of Schiller, Friedrich Schlegel (one of the founding-figures of German Romanticism), K. T. Körner, and, late in his life, Rückert, a poet who was to inspire many of Schubert's followers in the later Romantic era. One of his most important discoveries was the verse of Wilhelm Müller, whose texts Schubert was to use for his two great song-cycles *Winterreise* (Winter Journey) and *Die schöne Müllerin* (The Fair Maid of the Mill). Another important literary influence was Johann Herder, who helped bring the ballad back into fashion. However, Schubert found many of his poetic sources in the work of friends such as Franz von Schober and Johann Mayrhofer. They could not be considered top-ranking poets, but they were at least creating side by side with the composer who gave their work immortality.

Musical influences

Schubert's music stemmed, firstly, from his natural talent, secondly from the music of his background – the great musical city of Vienna and its rich inheritance of *ländler* (a lively folk-dance) and waltz, and thirdly from the works of his predecessors – those who touched his heart and mind. These included Mozart in particular, who had died in 1791 only some six years before Schubert was born and was already becoming something of a legend; Haydn who was living and working until Schubert was 12; and Beethoven, the great giant of Viennese music, who always dominated Schubert's life and work although the composer was too timid to make his acquaintance. The threads that make up Schubert's style clearly owe something to each of these.

But teenage geniuses are often most directly inspired by art on a lower level; some of the composers who guide Schubert's early steps are, in terms of their lasting value, hardly worth mentioning. Who has heard of Johann Rudolph Zumsteeg today? Yet he was to provide at least the working model for Schubert's early songs. He was a friend of Schiller whose melodramatic ballads he had set to music with what Haydn described as 'imagination and a fine sense of form'. Working in a similar early romantic vein was Johanne Friedrich Reichardt (who wrote over 700 songs, none of which is widely remembered) and Carl Friedrich Zelter, a close friend of Goethe who perhaps led Schubert some of the way toward the master.

Schubert's* Erlkönig *(The Erl-King), one of his most famous songs, turns Goethe's chilling tale of the supernatural into a moving portrayal of a child's fear and a father's anxiety. Moritz von Schwind, Schubert's painter friend, managed to visualize and capture the drama of the song (right).

Schubert's first masterpiece and his first Goethe setting was* Gretchen am Spinnrade *(Margaret at the Spinning-wheel) – (below). It is a remarkably profound rendering of Gretchen's grief and passion as she sits spinning, recalling her lost love. Her emotions are echoed in the faltering whirrings of the wheel, magically depicted by Schubert's piano part.

Moritz von Schwind 'Der Erlkönig'. München, Schackgalerie. Joachim Blauel/Artothek

Induno 'La Filatrice'. Genova, Galleria d'Arte Moderna di Nervi/Scala

We have no way of knowing how many apprentic songs Schubert may have written as a boy. The firs one that is listed in the standard catalogue of his work (compiled by Otto Erich Deutsch and first publishe in 1951) is *Hagars Klage* (Hagar's Lament) wit words by one Schücking, first published in 178 These words had already been set to music by Johan Zumsteeg in 1797 (the year Schubert was born) an Josef von Spaun tells us that Schubert started out, b way of exercise, simply to modernize Zumsteeg' version. But he got so carried away by his task that h went on to produce his own setting which h presented to his teacher, Salieri. This first survivin song is a remarkable foretaste of the future with dramatic piano accompaniment and an obvious fla for accommodating the human voice. If it is not masterpiece, it is nevertheless singable. Schube continued in this vein of heavy Romanticism discovering the poems of Schiller on the way, an gradually evolved his own distinctive style.

Early brilliance

In 1814 Schubert decided to give up teaching at hi father's school and to take the plunge as a full-tim composer. Much of his effort that year was put int song-writing and we can detect the first hints of th lyrical Schubert in *Der Abend* (Evening). His firs vocal masterpiece arrived the *Gretchen am Spinnrade* (Gretchen at the Spinning-wheel), th words taken from Goethe's *Faust.* The great Schuber singer Dietrich Fischer-Dieskau sees it as 'the birth c

e essential, the great Schubert Lied'. This was hubert's first association with the words of Goethe d he at last found the strength and flow that he eded to inspire him:

eine Ruh ist hin,/ Mein Herz ist schwer,/ Ich finde e nimmer/ Und nimmermehr (my peace of mind s gone/ my heart is heavy/ and I shall never ever find again)

ne young girl is distracted by the loss of her lover ne of the classic romantic situations) and as she ngs she spins her wheel. The accompaniment is the pinning-wheel itself, with its monotonous ovement, which Schubert skilfully varies as the girl's ngers falter or her sorrow deepens. Here is the amatic side of Schubert's song-writing first showing s true promise.

In 1814 he also made the acquaintance of Johann ayrhofer, who became his friend and room-mate, a lented poet with a shy, serious nature akin to hubert's. After Goethe, Mayrhofer was to be the et whose verse Schubert used most. 1815 was a uitful year in which he wrote no less than 145 songs. he contrasting sides of his genius are seen in such a ng as *Heidenröslein* (Little Rose of the Hedgerow), the lightest possible lyrical vein, and *Erlkönig* (The l-King) in the heavily dramatic mode. The first of ese uses a poem by Goethe:

h ein Knab ein Röslein stehn,/ Röslein auf der eiden (There was a boy who saw a rose blooming in e hedgerow)

Wilhelm Müller (below) wrote the 20 poems in Schubert's song cycle* Die schöne Müllerin *(The Fair Maid of the Mill) – (right). Shortly before his death, Müller had expressed the hope that some day a 'kindred spirit' would 'catch the melodies from my words and give me back my own'. He remained unaware that Schubert had already done precisely this.

Archiv für Kunst und Geschichte

The poem offers very obvious attractions to a composer, as it trips along to an impulsive meter. There was little that Schubert needed to do but summon up his natural Viennese tunefulness and probably in less than an hour the world had been given a natural gem that it was to treasure for ever.

In the *Erlkönig* Schubert found Goethe in superbly melodramatic mood: the father rides wildly through the night with his terrified child in his arms and they try to run the gauntlet of the ghostly Erl-King. It ends as morbidly as a young Romantic could desire:

Dem Vater grauset's, er reitet geschwind,/ Er hält in den Armen das ächzende Kind,/ Erreicht den Hof mit Mühe und Not;/ in seinen Armen das kind war tot. (The father shudders, he now rides fast,/In his arms he holds the groaning boy,/He reaches the farm with his last strength:/In his arms the child was dead.)

Schubert's accompaniment offers a comparison of the steady thud of the hooves, in triplets, as they race through the night and the swirling bass figures of the ghostly mists, combining to give a chilling sense of the supernatural. It is interesting to note that Schubert may have found his idea in part of the dungeon scene in Beethoven's *Fidelio,* which proceeds in a remarkably similar way. This in no way detracts from his own song. He accepts the possibilities that Beethoven suggests, but he transforms the idea into something essentially his own.

Little public recognition

At this time Schubert's songs were mainly intended for the enjoyment of a close circle of friends and they were sung and heard at evenings *(Schubertiaden)* that generally began with poetry readings, proceeded with music and ended with a visit to one of their favourite drinking haunts in the early hours of the morning. Schubert would bring along settings of poems by

Archiv für Kunst und Geschichte

H. Baldung Grien 'Knight, Death and the Maiden'. Paris, Louvre/Scala

Mayrhofer and his other friends and they would help him to choose poems by Goethe and other famous poets. It was during 1816 that Josef von Spaun thought it a good idea to send Goethe some of Schubert's settings of his poems. Schubert neatly copied out 16 of them and Spaun sent them with a letter saying (somewhat optimistically) that they were soon to be published in two volumes and asking for permission to dedicate them to Goethe. The volume was returned with not a word of encouragement or response from the great poet. Throughout his life, Goethe never acknowledged the existence of Schubert nor mentioned him in his letters and diaries.

1817 saw the production of another 60 songs, among them the dramatic *Der Tod und das Mädchen* (Death and the Maiden) with a theme that he was to use later in a quartet; the superbly modelled *An die Musik* (To Music); and the ineffably joyous *Die Forelle* (The Trout). It was also the year in which Schubert first met the famous singer and his future friend Johann Michael Vogl. Vogl at first was only mildly encouraging with regard to Schubert's songs, but he began to perform them regularly and soon became his greatest admirer. His fame allowed him to alter what he pleased but Schubert accepted his help, later writing: 'The way Vogl sings these things, and I accompany him – so that while the performance lasts we seem to be one – is a quite unheard-of novelty.'

Schubert's song* Der Tod und das Mädchen *(Death and the Maiden), composed in 1817, was one of his most popular at the* Schubertiaden. *This no doubt prompted him to write the D minor String Quartet, which, like 'The Trout', has a whole movement based on variations of the song.

While a host of minor composers were published in their lifetime, Schubert had great difficulties getting even his songs accepted. This allowed sharp businessmen, such as Diabelli, to exploit the desperate composer.* Heidenröslein *(Little Rose of the Hedgerow) – (right) was one of the gems that Diabelli virtually stole from him.

Here he shows how keenly he realized the importance of blending words and music – which was very much his special gift to the art of songwriting. It is interesting to note, too, that Schubert himself was a fairly accomplished pianist and singer. It is perhaps the fact that he rarely makes excessive demands on either his pianists or singers that has helped his songs to appear rather more accessible and enjoyable than most of the *Lieder* output of the 19th century.

Attempts to be published

Vogl was able to make a song like *Erlkönig* a popular favourite in Viennese circles and this encouraged Schubert to send it to the famous publishers, Breitkopf & Härtel, in Leipzig. They rejected it immediately without comment and, in fact, never published a note of Schubert in his lifetime, though they were later the publishers of his *Complete Works.* They added insult to injury by accidentally returning the manuscript to another composer called Franz Schubert who was a double-bass player in the Dresden Court orchestra. He wrote to the publishers indignantly disclaiming any connection with 'that sort of trash', utterly disgruntled that any other fellow had so misused his name. Schubert eventually got his manuscript back.

Others, however, were more discerning and his reputation as a songwriter steadily grew in his native city. His first song to be published was *Erlafsee* which appeared in a supplement to an almanac issued early in 1818. But it was only through the untiring efforts of his friends that his songs were published in any quantity, and this was not until 1821 after Vogl had had yet another great success with his singing of *Erlkönig* at a public concert at the Court Theatre. Sonnleithner, Hüttenbrenner and others got together and published the work privately, having it printed by Diabelli. Proceeding on a cautious sale or return basis they did quite well out of *Erlkönig,* published in April, followed by *Gretchen, Heidenröslein* and others and Schubert himself was quite well rewarded. He spoilt the whole arrangement, however, by taking it upon himself to sell his copyright to Diabelli for a down payment and, as a result, lost what could have been a steady regular income.

The two great song-cycles

The essence of Schubert is to be found in the two song-cycles (sequences of songs with a linking theme) that he wrote to poems by Wilhelm Müller – *Die schöne Müllerin* (The Fair Maid of the Mill) in 1823; and *Winterreise* (Winter Journey) in 1827. With the first it was a matter of joyful inspiration at a time when life still had an optimistic side. Calling on a friend one

Schäfers Klagelied.
Heidenröslein. Jägers Abendlied.
Meeres Stille von Goethe.
Für eine Singstimme
mit Begleitung des PIANO-FORTE in Musik gesetzt
und dem Wohlgebohrnen Herrn Herrn
IGNAZ EDLEN VON MOSEL
k.k. wirkl. Hofrath und Vice Director der k.k. Hoftheater,
hochachtungsvoll gewidmet
von
Franz Schubert
3tes Werk.
WIEN.
in Commission bey Cappi und Diabelli am Graben No. 1133.

day, Schubert picked up Müller's poems while waiting in the library. He was so excited by the ideas that it inspired in him that he went off, taking the book with him. Apologizing the next day, he showed his friend some of the songs he had already completed. Starting the sequence in May, Schubert left it for a while to complete his opera *Fierabras*. Then he was in hospital for a while where he started writing again. He finished the cycle by October.

The sequence is a naively simple story of love and lost love, of the young man who falls in love with a beautiful girl, loses her and drowns himself in the stream. It is this dancing brook, sometimes bright and sunny, finally dark and sad, that links the songs. It acts as a continuous background as the spinning-wheel did for *Gretchen*. The 'rippling movement', 'the running water' theme, pinpointed by Capell, comes into its own here. The sequence brought an instant reaction from Schubert. It took him back to the simple songs of his earlier days. Some he reshaped. *Daphne am Bach* of 1816 returns thinly disguised as *Wohin?*. Almost a third of the songs in the cycle are simple songs with repeated verses. The penultimate song *Der Müller und der Bach* moves from the folksong world of *Das Wandern* to add a poignant G minor accompaniment to the Miller's last song. Finally, the brook sings a lullaby to the dead lover, a song of repeated verses, tender yet complacent. Lovers come and go but the brook goes on for ever.

By 1827 Schubert was in his darkest and most sombre mood. Racked with pain, disappointed in his achievement, he hid himself away from his friends and found in Müller's sad, near-morbid *Winterreise* a reflection of his own despair. He reappeared to offer his friends a cycle of 'frightening songs'. They were much perturbed by the sadness and pessimism of what they heard. The only one that Schober could bring himself to praise was the lighter *Der Lindenbaum* (The Linden Tree). Schubert declared that these were his greatest songs and the world would come to see them as such. In one of the songs *Der Leiermann* (The Organ-Grinder) he must have been thinking of his own fate – the musician to whom nobody wanted to listen.

We have little or no hint from Schubert himself of what he thought of the art of songwriting or whether he actually gave the matter much thought. Where he does mention certain songs in his letters it is simply to say that he thought it fair or good or 'the best thing I have done' so far. Writing music was so natural to Schubert that the mechanics of it hardly bothered him. If he felt reasonably well and untroubled he wrote easily, but in darker moods composition became difficult. If he came to think of the *Winterreise* cycle as one of his finest achievements, it was simply because the songs therein were the hardest to achieve, written when his spirits were at their lowest ebb, a triumph in adversity. The joyful moments that prompted the simple beauty and warmth of *Die Forelle* must have also brought him great happiness.

Between February and October 1827, Schubert composed the 24 songs in the tragic* Winterreise *(Winter Journey) cycle on poems by Wilhelm Müller. The cycle is a heartfelt excursion into the depths of loneliness, reflected externally by a bleak winter landscape (below). The hapless lover abandons his warm home and wanders in utter desolation through the snowfilled night. His evolving emotions are charted in each song in one of Schubert's most disturbing and moving masterpieces.

Listener's guide

Any analysis of the life and times of a great composer cannot ignore his music, and the Listener's Guide *examines in detail some of Schubert's greatest and best-known works: 'The Trout' piano quintet, his Fifth Symphony and his Eighth or 'Unfinished' Symphony. The sections on specific aspects of musical development (for example, the development of* Lieder *or art-songs brought to perfection by Schubert) can be read along with the descriptions of the pieces of music as an examination of Schubert's musical achievements. However, for the fullest appreciation of this great composer's music, the programme notes are better read before going to a live performance or while listening to the recorded music. Suggestions for further listening are given in the text, and the Bibliography and short descriptions of the lives and works of contemporary composers suggest other areas of study should you wish to learn more about Schubert's life and times.*

Understanding music: orchestration

In his orchestration, Joseph Haydn (above) tried to create a clear and graceful sound, often emphasizing a single high melodic line over a distinct bass.

One of the most striking features of Classical and Romantic music is the predominance of the orchestra. It is as if, having discovered the possibilities of such a large and varied group of instruments, few serious composers could devote themselves to any other medium.

In the 18th century, orchestration was largely intended to produce a sound of grace and beauty. Generally, the higher instruments would play the melody while the lower-toned instruments would provide a rhythmic accompaniment, and the mid-range instruments would fill out the harmonies. Clearly, the best composers would introduce variations on this pattern, but it provided a solid base.

Another traditional feature of 18th century orchestration is the way string parts were often *doubled* by the woodwind – that is, they play the same part. Thus violins, the highest string instruments, double with flutes, the highest woodwinds, and it is this pairing that often plays the melody. Similarly, oboes might double with the second violins, clarinets with violas and bassoons with cello or double bass. Horns could provide a unifying blend.

Doubling became less popular towards the end of the 18th century and contrasting passages of wind alone, or passages where a solo woodwind emerged from the throng, were common.

During the 19th century, the emphasis of orchestration shifted. The composer used the orchestra not to produce a graceful sound but to create a particular effect. Music became dramatic, even pictorial – no doubt composers were influenced by the way orchestras in opera houses were used by composers like Weber and Rossini to create theatrical effects. Although few pieces are so unashamedly descriptive as Berlioz's *Symphonie Fantastique,* much Romantic orchestral music is remarkably vivid.

Musical colour

The idea of the colour of sound seemed particularly attractive and the orchestrator was often likened to the painter, blending colours to build up a picture. The particular sound of an instrument – its *timbre* – was described, as it still is, in terms of colour. A bassoon, for instance, is 'dark' in tone; a flute is 'light'. Harmonies, too, seemed to have colour – so much so that later Skryabin could describe the chord of C major as 'red'. Even the way the harmonies were arranged seemed to suggest a particular shade.

Similarly, the music could sound 'empty' or 'full'. To create an 'empty' sound, for instance, a composer would use just a few instruments, widely spaced in pitch – such as flute and bassoon.

By using the colour of particular instruments, harmonies and spacing and the sense of depth created by certain combinations of instruments, the composer could use the orchestra to paint a vivid picture.

It is important to bear in mind, though, that the composer also needed a detailed knowledge of the practical capabilities of all the instruments – and the players – if he was to use the orchestra to best effect. It is significant that some of the most dramatic changes in orchestration were encouraged by improvements in certain instruments. The 18th-century tradition of wind and string doubling, for instance, waned partly because the technical advances in woodwind design enabled flutes and clarinets to take a more positive part. Similarly, the development of valves made brass instruments considerably more versatile – some of the more strident passages of late Romantic orchestral music would not have been possible without valved brass.

Even the talent and character of the musicians in the orchestra played a significant part in orchestration – for many years violas, for instance, doubled with second violins simply because viola players were thought not to be up to a full part.

Ultimately, though, no amount of knowledge of colour effects and instrumental qualities can help the composer if he has no clear idea of the sound he wants from the orchestra. It is the quality of this idea that distinguishes the great composer of orchestral music from the mere orchestrator.

LISTENER'S GUIDE

Piano Quintet in A major, op. 114

The Piano Quintet is one of the most popular chamber works, and Schubert's first masterpiece in instrumental music.

The carefree charm and spontaneity of Schubert's Piano Quintet in A, better known to the world as the *Trout Quintet,* suggests that it was written in one of the happier periods of his short and troubled life. The beginning of 1818 saw him in a period when friends were exceptionally helpful and when it looked as though his music was to be given the opportunities and recognition it needed.

He received a small but regular income from his employment as music master to the two daughters of Count Esterházy and he also received commissions for a number of operettas.

During the summer of 1819 he took a walking tour in the mountains of Upper Austria with his new-found friend, the opera singer Michael Vogl. They stayed for some time in Vogl's home town, Steyr, beautifully situated at the meeting of two rivers, the Steyr and the Enns, about 90 miles to the west of Vienna. It was a picturesque town boasting a central square with houses dating back to the 15th century, and was known as a centre for manufacturing firearms.

Here Schubert took lodgings at the congenial home of Dr Schellmann, where he spent many happy hours playing the piano for song recitals, often of his own work, by his host's daughters and their friends. He was also invited to compose a piece of music for the local music society, organized and led by one of Schellmann's neighbours, an amateur cellist, Sylvester Paumgartner.

Schubert enthusiastically agreed to write the work to suit their and his musical capabilities, and he began at once writing the Piano Quintet in A and may even have completed one or two movements during the holiday. A variation movement was decided upon, to give the participants their virtuoso spots.

Herr von Stoller, at whose table Schubert took a daily meal, was an accomplished bass player, and his daughter Josephine was the inspiration and first performer of the piano part.

Paumgartner is credited with suggesting the melody of Schubert's song, *Die Forelle* (The Trout), as the theme of the work. *Die Forelle* was written in 1817, and set to the words of C. F. D. Schubart, a poet whose works Schubert often used.

When Schubert returned to Vienna at the end of the holiday, he added the final touches and the necessary polish to the work. It was sent back to the friends at Steyr and first performed by the Paumgartner ensemble in Steyr at the end of 1819.

First performance

The first performance of the world's most popular chamber work seems to have gone unheralded – it was simply a pleasant realization of the work among friends.

It took place in a musical drawing room on the second floor of Paumgartner's house at number 16 in the central square. Paumgartner is said to have given only a modest account of the cello part, while Josephine got through the demanding piano role fairly well. There is no evidence of what the local critics thought of it. Perhaps they reflected the view of the late J. A. Westrup, a Schubertian critic, who said that it 'is entertainment music from first to last, and should be listened to with simple unsophisticated enjoyment. To drink – even to talk – during a performance would not be a blasphemy'. His summary that it was 'holiday music for amateurs' is a narrow view to take of this lovely work, which many authorities describe quite simply as Schubert's first masterpiece in instrumental music. In view of its position in the Deutsch catalogue, D667 of 965, this might seem late for a first masterpiece to make its appearance, but it has to be remembered that Schubert was only 22 at the time of its composition.

Loss of original manuscript

The loss of the original manuscript is another of the minor tragedies which beset so much of Schubertian history. It is probable that Vogl arranged with Joseph Czerny of Vienna, for the publication of the Quintet, along with the Piano Sonata in A, and the work appeared in the spring of 1829. According to Albert Stadler, who had copied out the parts from Schubert's original for Paumgartner, Vogl had the manuscripts when Schubert died on 19 November, 1828. It is possible that he only had the fair copies made by Stadler, since the original draft was probably so rough it

A relaxed Schubert (above) wrote 'The Trout' quintet during the summer of 1819, while he was holidaying in the mountains of Upper Austria (left). The rolling hills, rippling streams and the beauty of the mountains inspired him and found expression in the essentially carefree piano quintet. The picturesque surroundings were not the only source of pleasure: at Schubert's lodgings were the daughters and friends of his host, Dr Schellmann. Many happy hours were spent together, resulting in the sunny holiday mood of the quintet (below).

was simply thrown away. Because of the loss we are unable to be certain in which order the work was composed, and so although credit is given to Paumgartner for suggesting the Trout theme, it is difficult to decide whether this was an afterthought when some of the work already existed, or whether it was a germinal idea. Certainly there is something of its spirit throughout.

Programme notes

Schubert's music is at its best when it is quirkish, moving into unexpected keys, but always based on a foundation of spontaneous song and using all of his gestures and tricks.

First movement – Allegro vivace
The upward moving arpeggios (chords on piano or harp which are performed spread out, with notes sounding in succession, usually moving upwards) with which the movement opens establish with great assurance several characteristics of the work. First they set the work in the bright and brisk key of A; a fact emphasized with stubborn resolution by the bass which has ten sustained bars on that note, following the clear opening chord by all the strings (viola, violin and bass). Secondly a pleasant refrain for the piano is outlined; this is introduced here and there throughout the movement. The third element is the lightness of the series of notes in triplets which are imposed on the basic four beats in the bar – this is a typical Schubert effect, used to portray water, essential here, to keep his trout alive. These light rushing notes are supplied as background by the piano for much of the time during the movement.

Early in the movement the violin, with assistance, begins stating the simple basic theme in A. Then Schubert, typically and

without any fuss or preparation, jumps straight into another key, F. The piano extends the basic theme and the strings take over the triplet movement. This gives a clear early indication of the later involvement with the Trout song, with its similarly upward flowing triplet accompaniment. It also makes it seem possible that Schubert had the theme in mind from the beginning.

The movement goes through several keys, notably a 'foreign' C major before the entrance of the second theme in E. This is often described as a 'Love duet' for cello and violin, the latter answering the former.

This is followed by a repeat of the first section. Then the strings take up a

Archiv für Kunst und Geschichte

Christian Friedrich Daniel Schubart, a minor German poet (left) whose poem Die Forelle *(The Trout) (right) Schubert set to music in 1817. The song was immediately popular, and its melody was used by Schubert as the theme of the Piano Quintet, written for his musical friends in Steyr.*

Archiv für Kunst und Geschichte

The bright quirkiness of the first movement suggests the brisk and sparkling movement of a clear, fast-flowing stream.

Hans Thoma 'Wiesenlandschaft', Bayerische Staatsgemäldesammlungen, Joachim Blauel/Artothek

repeated figure in C, from which they are dragged into E flat by the octaves of the piano. Here they stay, all unaware, it seems, that the work is supposed to be in A. Schubert gets out of this with a recapitulation at the end of the movement, which begins in D, and a tailpiece ending neatly in the home key of A.

All the key changes help to establish the wonderful changes of colour and flow that underlie the whole of this movement; suggesting the contrasting movement in the flow of a playful stream.

Second movement – Andante

The second movement is in two parts, each part containing three sections. The character and the balance of the work are well maintained and one of the remarkable things about the Trout Quintet, considering its light nature, is its consistency of character. The first section of the andante starts in the key of F with its main tune given out in octaves by the piano which,

Example 2

Andante

after a few bars, takes on an unexpected jigging nature with a dotted semiquaver rhythm. This feature and the triplets introduced soon after are kept as melodic motifs throughout to break up the otherwise smooth flow. At bar 24, just before the second strain is introduced, the work moves into F sharp minor and the piano adopts a flowing semiquaver accompaniment (the brook again) which it maintains throughout this section with the viola and cello introducing a tune reminiscent of an earlier Schubert work. At bar 36 a third tune is introduced in the key of D, the dotted rhythm is used by the strings and the piano accompanies in triplets. The three sections are developed, and lead to a briefly settled flow in G as the stream gathers momentum. Schubert follows this with one of the sudden changes that he could never resist. Having ended this setting out of tunes on a decided affirmation of G, he begins the recapitulation in A flat and the three sections are more or less repeated, but the keys take a parallel course – A flat, A minor and finally F – the key in which the movement started. But this is only reached after following an unexpected, yet in the end logical, course of key changes. None of these changes interrupts or disturbs the smooth, artless, almost naive progress of this beautiful movement; a deep and calm stretch of water after the turbulence of the first movement.

Third movement – Scherzo presto

The scherzo is a lively movement played in a fast tempo and with little sentimentality or grandiose elements. This third movement is a rather quirkish interlude which, while it does not change the character of the whole work, is almost a dance in 3/4 time. Or at least it would be if it were not given a trout-like, darting quality by its initial four-bar tune with a rather

Example 3

unexpected two-bars tagged on and then repeated by the piano. The whole movement has this eccentric character with suddenly emphasized long notes – in fact, were it not firmly entrenched in the 19th century it might be tempting to say that it has a ragtime flavour about it. Although the key signature remains A, the underlying key soon becomes C, with a second strain, which then moves into F major. The simple themes have been neatly contrived for some playful counterpoint. As with the old Minuet movements, the Scherzo has its trio.

This, as in most Schubert symphonies, is a smoothly tranquil section which is not, however, without ingenuity. To begin with the violin and viola act as a duo with their phrases answered by the piano playing a two-part role with the two hands moving in parallel. Then the cello and bass come in with their duet and, by the end, the piano has thickened out to a four-part harmony to balance the forces of the strings. As by now expected, Schubert satisfies his harmonic wanderlust with an excursion into B flat in the second half of the trip. The movement closes with the opening sections of the Scherzo exactly repeated.

Fourth movement – Theme and Variations (Andantino)

At last Schubert introduces the immortal theme, known so well as *The Trout,* slightly modified from its original song form (Schubert wrote at least five different versions not only slightly changing the shape of the theme but varying its markings between *poco allegro* and *moderato*). The quintet version is rather more refined and steadier than the general song form, its rhythm altered by dotted notes and its key changed from the D flat of the song (a) to the less devious D (b) which also allies it more naturally to the overall A major tonality of the whole work.

Example 4

Firstly the theme is simply stated, *andantino,* by the strings alone. In variation I the piano takes over in a decorated form with the hands playing treble clef octaves against little flurries from the violin and cello, a rippling

Understanding music: Lieder (song)

Lieder (pronounced *leeder*) is the German word, meaning 'songs'. Generally speaking, all solo songs in German with piano accompaniment may be called Lieder. But specifically, especially in the English-speaking world, the term has come to be indelibly linked with the German Romantic period of the 1800s, and the kind of *art-song* (as distinct from folk-song) brought to perfection by Franz Schubert.

Songs are said to be *strophic,* in which the verses are all set to the same tune throughout, as in hymns; or *through-composed* (non-strophic), in which the music moves forward continuously to follow the course of the words. Schubert used both these forms in his Lieder. Sometimes he merely modified the strophic form. In *Der Wegweiser* ('The Sign Post'), for example, he kept the same melody throughout but shifted the middle section of the song into the minor key.

Schubert's natural successor in the field of Lieder was Robert Schumann (1810–56). In 1840 Schumann turned from piano works to Lieder, and in that year alone he composed nearly 150 of his total of 200 songs. Out of these his masterpiece is generally acknowledged to be *Dichterliebe* ('Poet's Love'), a cycle of 16 songs based on poems by Heinrich Heine. This was a time when Schumann was going to law to obtain permission to marry Clara Wieck against her father's wishes. It is not surprising that Heine's poems, redolent with images of unrequited love, should fuel Schumann's own disturbed emotions. Schumann was meticulous in his treatment of verbal values. In his Lieder the text is not only clearly projected but emphasized with subtle touches of rhythm, melody, harmony, and texture.

Later in the 1800s, Johannes Brahms (1833–97) continued and added lustre to the great Lieder tradition which was inaugurated by Schubert. Brahms composed in this medium with great skill and charm at various intervals throughout his working life. He wrote more than 260 Lieder altogether, and freely acknowledged Schubert as his model. A strong element of folksong is evident in many of his compositions, which are treated for the most part in strophic fashion. Although there is passion in the Lieder, this feeling seems to be more controlled and less impulsive than it is in Schumann's works. Brahms's artful melodies betray an affection for the piano that

The first impression the quintet gives is of lightness and spontaneity, but in the second movement the gaiety gives way to a more contemplative mood. The slowness of part of the movement hints at deeper and calmer water (left), after the turbulence of the earlier rapids.

Karinger 'Mountain Landscape' Ljubljana, Narodna Galerija/Scala

Moritz von Schwind 'Das Knaben Wunderhorn'. Joachim Blauel/Artothek

sometimes threatens to diminish the voice. Perhaps the greatest of his Lieder are the *Vier ernste Gesange* ('Four Serious Songs'). These are based on Biblical texts and are replete with intense but restrained emotion.

The last of the great Lieder writers of the 1800s was Hugo Wolf (1860–1903). He chose his poets carefully – Michelangelo, Goethe, Eichendorff, and translations of Italian and Spanish poets. His enthusiasm for the music of Richard Wagner is reflected in a kind of equality between poetry and music which is often concentrated in single musical phrases of great intensity.

Gustav Mahler carried the tradition of the German *Lied* into the present century. He was seminal in his use of the orchestra as accompaniment to the singer, making available an increased palette of colour and sound. The *Des Knaben Wunderhorn* settings are among his masterpieces. In these simple, heart-felt songs, Mahler uses folk poems as a vehicle for his own intensely personal vision and feelings. The cycle *Kindertötenlieder* (Songs on the Death of Children), displays his mastery of orchestral settings in songs of compelling drama and pathos.

Moritz von Schwind's illustration to* Des Knaben Wunderhorn *(left).

Karl Spitzweg 'Der Angler'. Privatbesitz Konsul Dr. Grupp, Burladingen. Joachim Blauel/Artothek

background from the viola and a light *pizzicato* (instruction to player that strings are to be plucked) bass. In variation 2 the violin and viola have the tune with the piano echoing them. In variation 3 the strings embellish the tune between them (even the bass having a contribution to make) while the piano darts along gaily with 16 notes to the bar. The style of the variations is conventional. In variation 4 the bass player is given his great chance both to embellish the tune and indulge in cumbersome triplets. He is not actually trusted to do it on his own but, as in much orchestral writing of the time, finds the cello more or less doubling his role while the rest of the quintet provide a dramatic background.

All have now moved into D minor. Variation 5 hovers between D minor and B flat with everyone moving as far away from the tune as they possibly can without actually relinquishing a hold on it – a perfect approach to what is really variation 6 (though it simply runs on in the score) now presenting us with the straightforward tune (cello) and the piano accompaniment more or less as in the song, as a serene finale to the movement. The tempo of the song is even restored here to an approximate *allegretto* (not as lively as an allegro). This bald statement of a tune is curiously satisfying and fulfilling as if the whole work was waiting for this moment, so divine in its simplicity. We can at least imagine that a hint of it was always there even if the whole idea was something of an afterthought. The movement has often been criticized for its conventionality, its lack of a grand conception. Nonetheless there is a pleasant 'rightness' about it and its most telling touch (variation 6) is the simplest and least contrived of all.

Fifth movement – Allegro giusto

Since Sylvester Paumgartner had specifically requested that the fourth movement be a set of variations on his favourite of Schubert's songs, Schubert added a fifth one. The standard number of movements in a Quintet is four: clearly, both Schubert and Paumgartner did not regard the 'Theme and Variations' movement as a

'And that fellow with the rod thinks they can't see him!' The words of* Die Forelle *capture the wily nature of the trout.

Gustave Courbet 'The Trout'. Zürich, Kunsthaus/Scala

suitable finale to the work. This finale is heralded by a commanding E. It is in two parts, like the slow movement, the first part starting in the conventional home key of A major, with this theme as its basis.

The sprightly theme, mainly in A with minor excursions into G; the second subject is in D. As in the slow movement the second half is simply ideas thrust together and happily finding they get on well. It has been described as a lazy ending to the work; but it is nonetheless exuberant and constantly mobile. And if the music is a delight in itself there is little hardship in hearing it twice. The words of the English translation of the song are a good guide to an imaginative appreciation of the music.

Jolly little beast, trout. Nimbler than we are, for all our arms and legs. Wily as can be, too. They can spell 'Angler' as well as most folk. And that fellow with the rod thinks they can't see him. Ha! now he says he'll be wily too. He's stirring the water up; but it takes more than that to bear a trout. No, I'm wrong. If he hasn't landed one!

The charm of the Trout Quintet is its inconsequential and inspirational mood. There are those serious musical fishers who would like to capture the Trout and dissect it; but its would-be captors are thwarted in the quintet, and the wily fish escapes their hooks. Those of not so serious a leaning have been able to enjoy Schubert at his most melodious and open-hearted throughout this friendly work.

In the song, the trout is landed (below) but in the quintet the trout escapes the hook and swims to outwit many an angler.

Great interpreters

Clifford Curzon (pianist)
Sir Clifford Curzon has long been regarded as among the élite of 20th century pianists. He died in 1982 at the age of 73, after being knighted in 1977. Born in 1909, he started at the Royal Academy at the age of 12. His playing soon won him many awards, including the McFarren Gold Medal. Having met Sir Henry Wood, he gave his first public concert at the Queen's Hall under the great man's baton, and was subsequently helped and guided by him in the early stages of his career.

By 1926, he was teaching at the Royal Academy; then, in 1928, he departed for Europe and more intense study. In Berlin, he spent two years under the tuition of the renowned virtuoso Artur Schnabel, and Curzon himself was later to testify to the profound effect Schnabel's presence and teachings had on him. After Berlin, Curzon travelled on to Paris for training with the legendary Nadia Boulanger, as well as Wanda Landowska. By the time he returned to England in 1932 he was ready for the life of a concert pianist, and for the years remaining before World War II he travelled constantly throughout Europe. In 1939 he made his first tour of America.

Sir Clifford Curzon, one of the great pianists of the 20th century, noted for his intellectual approach and sensitive touch.

After the War his stature continued to grow as he appeared with virtually every major orchestra, and in every major musical centre, both sides of the Atlantic, gaining a reputation among his fellow musicians as well as the general public that was second to none. By the early 50s he had had works written for and dedicated to him, and had given first performances of important new works by British composers.

For the rest of his life, Curzon alternated between concert performances and extended sabbaticals for further musical studies. His repertoire became increasingly concentrated on the classical period, and, as performances became less frequent, each was regarded more by music lovers.

Curzon was a player whose style was founded on the qualities of balance and sensitivity. Gifted with superb touch on the piano, his intellectually incisive approach and dignity of execution made for a rich musical feast when he played. Unfortunately, he left a very small recorded legacy, for he was a perfectionist and was very seldom satisfied with his own playing, and vetoed many record projects.

The Vienna Octet
The Octet, founded by Willi Boskovsky, quickly established a reputation as an examplary chamber group. Boskovsky is a violinist of note and is a leading conductor of the music of the Strauss family.

FURTHER LISTENING

Schubert Chamber Music and Lieder
String Quintet in C Major, D.956 (1828)
The D.956 quintet is generally regarded as Schubert's finest achievement in chamber music. The first two movements reach a rare nobility and depth through the exquisite voicings of the strings and the radiant beauty of melody and counter-melody. In the slow movement in particular there are lines of haunting simplicity and delicacy. The rest of the work shows no loss of inspiration but rather a change of mood into typically playful and engaging textures.

Die Schöne Müllerin, D.795 (1823)
Schubert didn't merely write great *lieder* (songs): he wrote great music in the form of lieder. His mastery of the art of bringing the most sympathetic musical rendering to poetry was complete. This cycle (the English translation is *The Fair Maid of the Mill*) tells the story of a mill-boy's unrequited love, and charts his progress from hope to fulfilment, then on to despair and death. Each of the 20 songs in the cycle captures one moment in this course.

Winterreise, D.911 (1827)
Schubert's second and last song-cycle was written just a year before his death, and shows a profound concern with intense personal loneliness and loss. The winter journey *(Winterreise)* of the rejected young man is indelibly etched in 24 songs. The subtle construction and the uncanny reflection of the poet's meaning in each song, places every one of them on the level of a masterpiece making the cycle as a whole an intensely moving experience.

LISTENER'S GUIDE

Symphonies nos. 5 and 8

Schubert composed his Fifth Symphony at the age of 19, and it positively bubbles over with youthful gaiety. The 'Unfinished', no. 8, is a relatively mature work of exquisite lyrical beauty and intensity.

Bildarchiv Preussischer Kulturbesitz

Schubert at the age of 16 (above), in the year that he composed his First Symphony. In the next three years an amazing quantity of music poured from his pen, culminating in the delightful Fifth Symphony of autumn 1816.

Symphony no. 5

If Franz Schubert had not begun early as a symphonist, we could hardly have had the nine he gave us. He reached that number in 1828, the year of his tragically untimely death at the age of 31. Like his beloved Mozart – but unlike Brahms or Bruckner, who were slow starters – Schubert took to symphonic writing naturally. His First Symphony was played by the Imperial Choir School orchestra in Vienna during, or soon after, the month of his leaving school, October 1813. Having written one symphony, the youthful composer seems to have taken to the form at once, composing with typical haste and lack of introspection. He produced a symphony in each of the following years, 1814 and 1815, while in 1816 he composed two. The Fifth Symphony was completed in September 1816, although it was not performed until 13 years after his death.

In its youthful spontaneity and enchanting melodies, Schubert's Fifth Symphony conjures up the light, pastoral world of the 18th century (left). That it has been described as 'Mozartian', is, as one critic suggests, to pay Mozart (below) a compliment.

Museen der Stadt Wien

A youthful symphonic masterpiece

Schubert was 19 when he composed his Fifth Symphony, and the music shows it. Not in any lack of skill – musically this young man was highly experienced – but because of its essentially youthful gaiety.

However, the year or so that led up to the writing of the Fifth Symphony seems to have been artistically challenging. Indeed, Alfred Einstein (in his book on Schubert) calls it a 'year of indecision'. Schubert was familiar with the symphonies of two very different composers, Mozart and Beethoven. His early symphonies had modelled themselves all too clearly on these masters, and were successful compositions as such. But now he needed somehow to discover his own individual voice. He had already done so in other areas of music – for example in the field of song, where he had produced such wholly personal masterworks as *Gretchen am Spinnrade* ('Gretchen at the Spinning Wheel') and *Erlkönig* ('The Erl King'). But by 1816 he had not yet found a way to be entirely himself in a large-scale work.

The composer himself seems to have known this, for after his Beethoven-like Fourth Symphony in April 1816, he may have decided that his own path lay in a very different direction. For it is Mozart, above all, whose spirit seems to preside over the Fifth Symphony which Schubert began as soon as he had laid the Fourth to rest. He finished it three months later. Yet this is now Mozart seen through Schubert's eyes (or heard through his ears). The paradox is illustrated by the fact that some people think that the very places which most recall Mozart are the most inspired, and the most individual to the composer.

Programme notes

The Fifth Symphony is the shortest among Schubert's youthful six (all written before the age of 21), and is scored for a smallish orchestra of one flute, two each of oboes, bassoons and horns, and strings. At one time it used to be called 'the symphony without trumpets and drums', and we may note that there are no clarinets in the orchestra either.

First movement – Allegro

The first movement has a charm and spontaneity which are typical of Schubert. It begins briskly yet softly: the first theme, introduced by woodwind and a little downward scale on violins, is as gracefully playful as a kitten:

Example 1

violins

pp

One commentator (Mosco Carner) says that the 'impudence' of this tune originates from Viennese street songs. Indeed it makes a fitting opening to what has often been described as 'Schubert's most Viennese symphony'. The upward figure is soon turned upside-down in a flute-violins dialogue, and the little downward run recurs, too, several times. Suddenly the whole orchestra, *forte* (loudly), plays an upward figure derived from the first theme, and the music proceeds quite purposefully and yet playfully to the second theme. This theme is echoed by the flute and oboe, and the music then bounds along toward the end of the exposition section, which has fulfilled its function of stating the main themes of the movement. Notice the little changes from major to minor – from a light to a slightly darker mood – which are typical of Schubert. The exposition ends with two vigorous chords and is then repeated, complete, in the 'classical' symphonic tradition.

Now comes the so-called 'development section'; we hear the music of the opening section once again, yet in a different guise: it is the introduction to the first theme rather than the theme itself which now occupies the composer, as the music moves through various quite remote keys. This is played softly, but leads to louder passages and what appears to be a new tune: it derives, however, from the second theme. The music calms down, for the *recapitulation* (restatement section) and our first theme (Example 1) reappears, this time slightly unconventionally, in a different key: E flat major. The second theme, though approached differently from

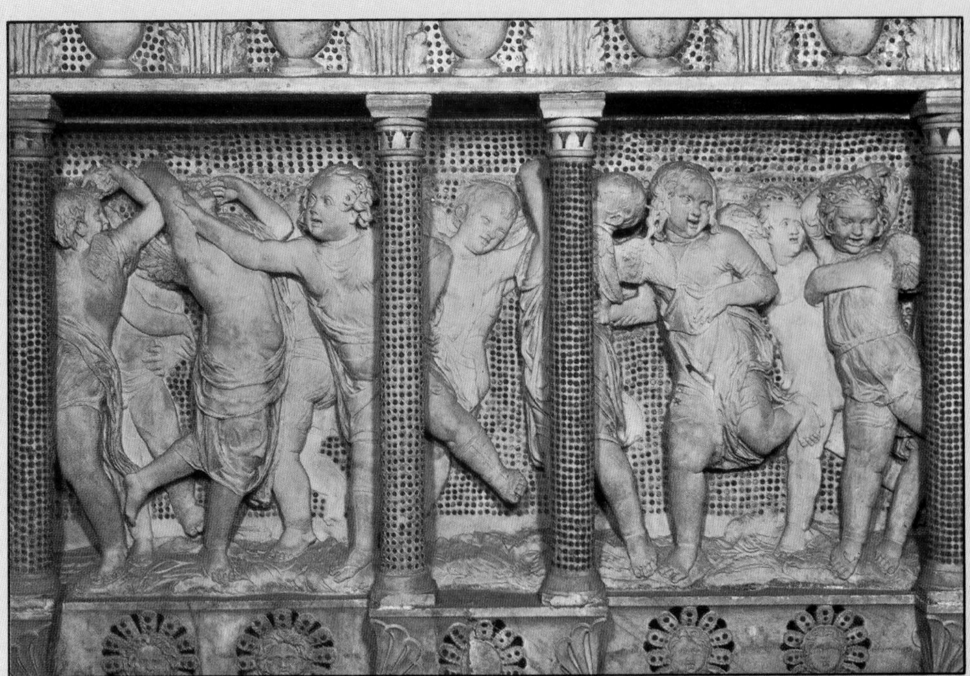

The playful, carefree mood of the first movement finds a parallel in Donatello's irresistibly light-hearted frieze (right).

The first theme, which in its 'cheekiness' seems to reflect the character of songs of the Viennese streets (below), makes a fitting opening to Schubert's most 'Viennese' Symphony.

before, is familiar enough when it appears. The *coda* (or closing section) features upward-rushing scales and brings the movement to a bright, boisterous close.

Second movement – Andante con moto
The Andante con moto is song-like and for at least one commentator suggests 'the peace and beauty of a pastoral summer's evening'. Many critics have mentioned Mozart, but some at least have found features of the harmony – the chord and key sequences – that are wholly typical of Schubert, as are the 'grace and sweetness' of the whole.

The lovely, song-like second movement suggests the beauty and tranquillity of a summer's evening in the country – a mood perfectly captured in John Linnell's painting (below).

The movement begins with the leisurely deployment of a lovely violin melody – at times *counterpointed* (matched with a similarly contoured melody) by the flute. Soon, however, comes a strange change of key, to C flat major, that could never have occurred in Mozart: a new tune is introduced here in the form of a dialogue between violins and woodwind. Then, via several changes of key and mood, Schubert gradually leads us back to the main opening theme (strings alone), which is then presented in a florid variation, ie. with extra decorative notes. Finally the first theme returns to bring the movement to a gentle close.

Victoria and Albert Museum/Scala

Third movement – Minuet: Allegro molto
This fresh and vivacious movement is brisk for a minuet, which originally, at least, was a rather stately dance, but in other respects it is quite traditional. Its striking and rather stern first theme has *tutti* (full orchestra) phrases alternating with gentler ones played by the violins. In the second section, flute, oboe, violins and low strings toss back and forth the first couple of bars of the theme over a repeated-chord accompaniment. Each of these two sections of the minuet are repeated. Then comes the *trio* (central part) of the movement, far gentler and smoother, although its lilting tune may well be derived from the striding opening theme. At one point the flute and oboe imitate the violins' tune at two bars' distance in a leader-and-follower manner. After that comes a *da capo* (in which the opening two sections are played over again stopping short at the point where the trio is reached).

Fourth movement – Allegro vivace
'Pure Haydn', said Einstein of the finale. Indeed, in this last movement Schubert seems to look affectionately back towards the 'classical' 18th century. Like the first movement, it is in sonata form: two themes or 'subjects' are stated (exposition section), developed and then restated (recapitulation). The dancing first theme ends with a little figure, innocent in itself, which is to play an important part in the music. Indeed, it instantly gives rise to a second tune, led off by the flute and oboe, before returning to be repeated. A new idea, alternating long notes and rushing string scales, all played loudly, now leads to a brief pause which is followed by a second theme of great charm:

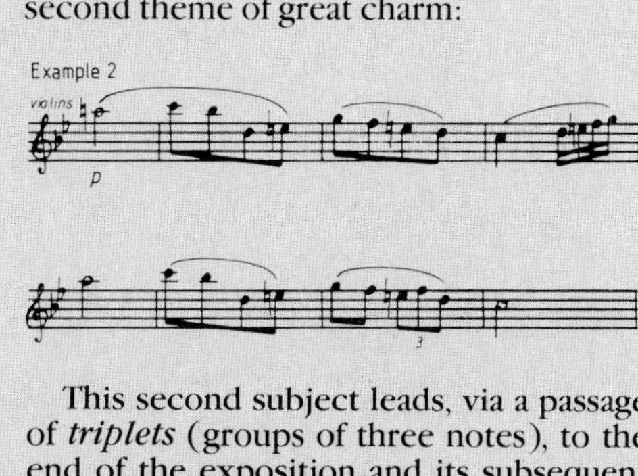

This second subject leads, via a passage of *triplets* (groups of three notes), to the end of the exposition and its subsequent repeat – a repeat which is sometimes omitted in performance. The development continues the busy inventiveness of this playful yet energetic finale. Fragments of the first theme are tossed about in a range of keys. Finally the home key of B flat major is once again reached – note the pause on a full-orchestral chord – and the first theme launches the recapitulation. With some compression we arrive at the second theme, after which all is much as before to bring the symphony to a vivid conclusion.

Symphony no. 8 ('Unfinished')

Despite its name, the 'Unfinished' Symphony in B minor, which we call no. 8, has been a repertory piece since its first performance in 1865. For although it has just two complete movements, they *are* complete, with Schubert's own detailed orchestration. Not only this, they contain some of his most beautiful and expressive music. Strangest of all, though the work ends in the 'wrong' key of E major, and we know that the composer intended to continue it with a scherzo (and surely a finale, too), it does not actually sound incomplete in the sense of leaving us unsatisfied.

Programme notes

Schubert completed his two movements of the 'Unfinished' Symphony at the end of October 1822. Then, having worked with his usual haste, he put them aside to begin work on his *Wanderer Fantasy*. During the following year, he gave the score away to his friend Josef Hüttenbrenner. Nobody knows why he parted with an incomplete work, although for a century musicians have racked their brains to find an answer. He certainly worked on his Scherzo third movement, reaching the central trio section in a piano sketch and something considerably less than this in orchestrated form. However, when his mind turned once again to symphonic writing, it was another work altogether that emerged; the 'Great' C major Symphony in the year of his death, 1828.

First movement – Allegro moderato

The passionately intense first movement begins with eight very soft bars for cellos and basses:

These serve as an introduction, and do indeed lead to the first subject, but will prove to be much more than this, yielding thematic material of great power. The first subject is, nevertheless, the gentle, almost twilight tune which we now hear played by the oboe and clarinet in unison over a rustling string accompaniment. The music builds to a climax, until, breaking the flow, it arrives at a long, sustained note on bassoons and horns. Now occurs Schubert's masterstroke: an enchanting, warmly expressive melody is played first by the cellos and then the violins. But after a mere 18 bars it suddenly stops and there is a moment of complete silence. Fierce *tutti* (full orchestra) chords break in and change the mood, and though after a few bars the second theme resurfaces, it is only at first in fragments, agitated where before all had been smooth. It seems that the latent unrest of the Symphony's opening has erupted, and that the calm can now never be fully restored. Nevertheless, five *pizzicato* (plucked) string notes descend slowly for the repeat of the exposition – all the music that we have heard until now.

The development section begins with the same music that opened the Symphony (Example 3), though now in a new key: E minor. The theme creeps forward mysteriously, building towards a violent climax, in which harsh chords, played *fortissimo* (very loudly) alternate with the offbeat accompanying chords, played *piano* (softly), of the second subject.

Now the development pursues its stormy way. The mysterious opening bars (Example 3) are thundered out by the whole orchestra, breaking up into fragments thereafter. The strings rush in furiously while wind and timpani play a pounding dotted rhythm. The climax of this development – which has been called a 'symphonic battle' – now occurs.

The wild music soon subsides towards the recapitulation section of the movement. The rustling strings and oboe-clarinet theme are restated, with modification only as is needed to give us the second subject – that sublime melody – (cellos as before) in a different key, D major. Schubert, by a brilliant formal stroke, extends it by an extra four bars at the point where, in the exposition, it was interrupted: the extra bars move us into

Turner's* Norham Castle at Sunrise *(right) evokes the same mysterious, dreamy mood that pervades the 'Unfinished' Symphony – particularly the gentler second movement, which ends on a note of utter serenity.

Gesellschaft der Musikfreunde

Schubert began working on the third movement, a Scherzo, completing the first page but only beginning the next (above). Why he abandoned the work at this point remains a mystery.

The Tate Gallery, London

the 'home' key of the Symphony, B minor, for the fierce tutti chords. And so, regularly, onwards to the pizzicato, descending strings that mark the end of the recapitulation.

Finally the closing section of the movement, or 'coda' begins rather like the development, rising fairly swiftly to a fortissimo climax. But this drops at once to its soft opposite, *pianissimo* (very softly) as the oboe and clarinet mournfully intone the opening bars of the Symphony. They are echoed by the full orchestra and the music subsides once again briefly before four loud assertive chords bring the movement to a close.

Second movement – Andante con moto

Schubert begins the slower second movement in the key of E major: for Mosco Carner, this is Schubert's key for 'peacefulness, dreamy contemplation, quiet resignation, pastoral feelings'. And the Andante con moto has all the lyrical beauty of the first movement, with perhaps an added poetry and depth. A brief prelude, for horns and bassoons over plucked basses, ushers in the main melody – a tune of wonderful serenity. The gentle mood is sustained for only a little while, however. There ensues what has been called 'a fortissimo passage of a processional nature' (wind over march-like strings) whose melody clearly derives from the violins' opening theme which then quietly reasserts itself.

Now Schubert introduces his second main melody. A quiet repeated-chord accompaniment on the strings supports a plaintive yet caressing tune which is played by the clarinet and which is then taken over by the oboe. This, like the first theme, has a little pendant:

Louvre/Michael Holford

The 'Unfinished' Symphony is often referred to as 'the torso'. For, just like a Greek torso (above) it is incomplete, but this in no way detracts from its beauty.

Example 4

Suddenly, this second melody bursts out fortissimo in the orchestral bass and the music moves fiercely towards a new key, D major, and an abrupt softening in tone; the cellos and basses play a melodic line deriving from the second (clarinet) theme, while the violins mimic them, loosely, at a bar's distance. This passage, of 'exquisite poetry', leads into the recapitulation.

Finally we reach the coda, which is of exceptional beauty. Fragments of the first theme seem to bid us a reluctant and loving farewell; the plucked cellos and basses are still there, and so are the 'lonely' soaring violin lines. The dynamic level is *ppp,* barely a whisper yet still expressive. On a note of the utmost serenity, the Symphony sinks into silence.

Was the Symphony 'Unfinished'?

It has been suggested that Schubert's Symphony no. 8 is not incomplete at all, simply a work conceived in two movements, like a few of Beethoven's piano sonatas. But this is most unlikely as we have Schubert's sketch of a third movement, a scherzo, with an orchestrated page written on the back of the last page of the Andante con moto. A second theory, that Schubert did, in fact, complete the Symphony but that the last two movements were then either lost or destroyed, seems now disproved by a discovery of the scholar Dr Christa Landon in Vienna, published in 1969. She found a second page of the composer's orchestral score of the third movement (the Scherzo). The page is incomplete, and it seems certain that Schubert removed it before sending the two-movement Symphony to Josef Hüttenbrenner.

Why then did Schubert never complete the work? Maurice Brown suggests that Schubert's inability to finish the Symphony may have been connected with the events that led to his illness at the end of 1822. To a sensitive young man like Schubert, he argues, the association of his illness with the Symphony may have made a return to it distressing. Indeed, the scholar Mosco Carner reminds us that the key of the 'Unfinished' Symphony, B minor, was in Schubert's time considered 'dark' in character. Its use was rare in a major work, and no symphony by Haydn, Mozart or Beethoven is in that key. He notes that Schubert's songs in the key of B minor seem to have texts expressing longing, or even grief.

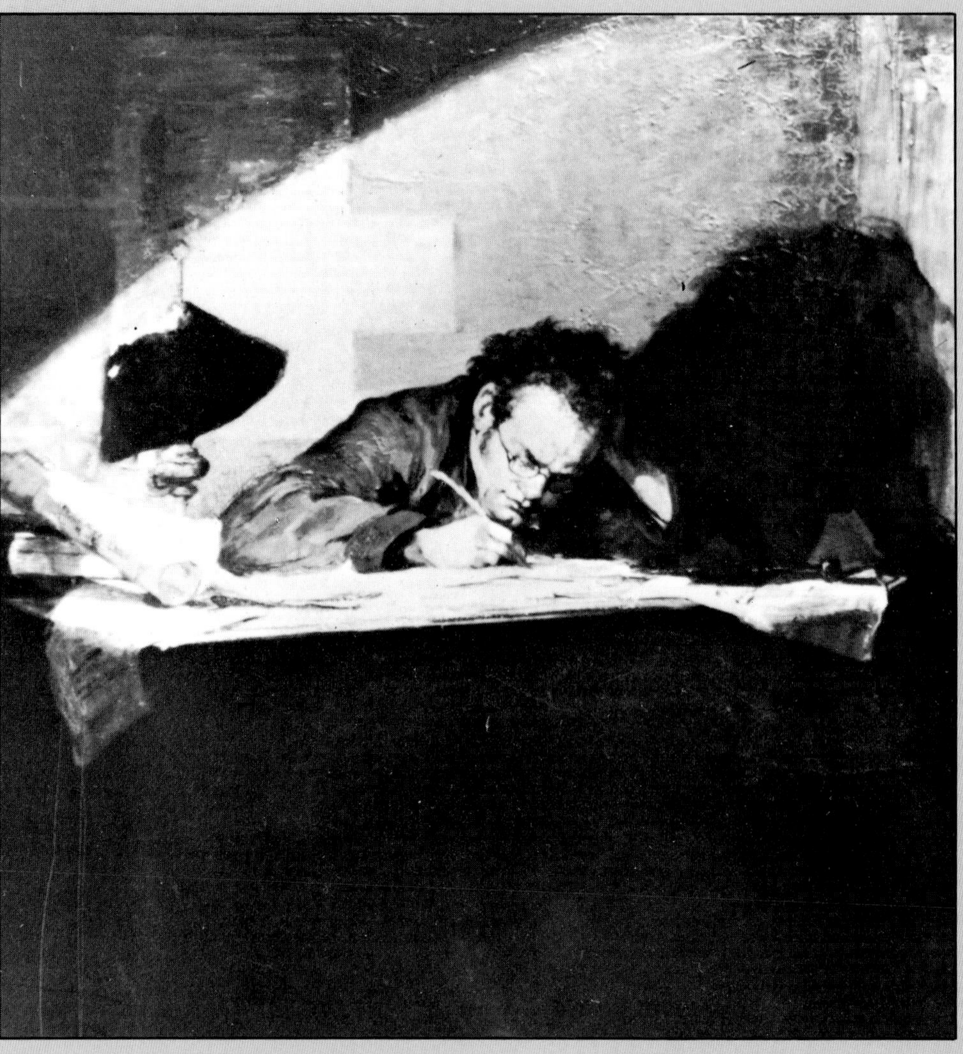

Schubert composed at a frantic speed (above), unhindered by reflection. Perhaps this is why he never returned to an unfinished work.

Abandoned

Perhaps the most convincing line of thought, however, is that offered by Hans Gals. He argues that Schubert abandoned the 'Unfinished' Symphony for the same reason that he left many other works incomplete: because difficulties had arisen and he eventually lost pleasure in the work. Schubert, it seems, worked happily and at an almost frantic speed, but when he reached a stumbling block he did not have the patience to wait for fresh inspiration. The increasing sparseness of the sketch for the Scherzo suggests a growing reluctance to continue with the Symphony. Having written two magnificent movements of extreme beauty, Schubert laid the work aside. And, never in his life did he return to an unfinished work. Realizing, perhaps, how great the work could have been, he gave the manuscript away, unable to live with the disappointment.

Now, and more briefly, to the known historical facts. The two completed movements of the Symphony are dated 30 October, 1822. In the following year Schubert sent the score to his friend Anselm Hüttenbrenner, via the latter's brother Josef, with the idea (apparently proven) that it should be presented to the Styrian Music Society with which Hüttenbrenner was associated and which had just granted Schubert honorary membership in recognition of his services to music. But, unbelievably, Hüttenbrenner kept the score to himself for over 40 years. Maybe, being the second-rate composer that he was, Anselm had grown jealous of Schubert's success.

Finally, however, in 1865, the elderly musician was persuaded to hand it over to Johann Herbeck, the conductor of the Vienna Philharmonic Orchestra. However, Anselm only gave up this musical treasure on condition that one of his works would be performed with it. Herbeck duly performed the works in Vienna on 17 December 1865, and Schubert's Symphony was published the following year. It was greeted with rapturous applause by audience and critics alike, while Anselm's work was largely ignored. It was not until about 20 years had passed that the nickname 'Unfinished' became attached to the work.

Schubert sent the Symphony to 'crafty-eyed' Anselm Hüttenbrenner (above), who kept it for over 40 years, and was at one time suspected of having destroyed the last two movements.

Great interpreters

Berlin Philharmonic Orchestra

In 1982 the BPO celebrated its centenary, and it is a remarkable fact that for most of its life it has been a top-flight orchestra.

In 1882, 54 musicians left the Bilsesche Kapelle to organize their own Philharmonic. Within a short space of time, guest conductors of the highest quality were being attracted to lead the orchestra. These included the composers Brahms, Tchaikovsky and Richard Strauss. From this point on, the BPO was priviledged with a long line of great chief conductors. After the legendary von Bülow, Arthur Nikisch led from 1895 to 1922.

In 1922 Wilhelm Fürtwangler succeeded Nikisch. One of this century's greatest conductors, he led the orchestra to even greater heights of interpretation: even during the Nazification of Germany, its standards of performance never faltered. After an interlude of two years, he led the orchestra until his death in 1954, when he was succeeded by Herbert von Karajan.

Under von Karajan, the orchestra's prestige has reached its zenith. Together they have performed and recorded virtually the entire popular classical repertoire. Von Karajan continues to lead the BPO, and both are pre-eminent.

Karl Böhm (guest conductor)

Karl Böhm has led the BPO as guest conductor for recordings of the complete symphonies of both Mozart and Schubert, and in performances and recordings he shows a complete grasp of two very different works. With the Fifth, Böhm uncovers its great poise and charm.

With the more profound 'Unfinished', Böhm's great depth and wisdom become immediately apparent. One of Böhm's greatest qualities was his ability to allow music to reveal its innermost character by setting tempos that were absolutely right, providing interpretation at the highest possible level.

FURTHER LISTENING

Symphony no. 9 in C major ('The Great') D.944
As with most of Schubert's output, his last symphony had to wait a considerable length of time – over ten years – for its first performance, and much longer than that before its true worth was seen. It projects a panorama as deep and broad as that of Beethoven's symphonies, yet remains essentially Schubertian – serene rather than epic in character. Today it stands as the crowning achievement in Schubert's orchestral canon.

***Rosamunde* (Incidental music), D.797**
Schubert's music for the stage has, by and large, never won the popular acceptance of his other works. But the Incidental music to the play *Rosamunde* is a happy exception. Written soon after the classic *Die Schöne Müllerin* ('The Fair Maid of the Mill') song-cycle, it displays all the melodic charm and beauty of the mature Schubert, rendered in a lively orchestral setting.

Impromptus (3 Series, D.899, D.935, D.946)
These pieces, short and unassuming as they may at first seem, are at the centre of the composer's pianistic achievement. Written initially in answer to a publisher's request for attractive piano music with only moderate technical demands, and not even titled by Schubert, they deliver a profusion of musical riches. Along with a few of his most characteristic melodies, these pieces also exhibit inspired musical reasoning.

In the background

Scientists still argue about which contributes most to our personalities, talents and behaviour: the inheritance of our genes or the influence of our environment. However, it is undeniable that we cannot help being affected to some extent by our surroundings, both in the narrow sense of our personal backgrounds and in the global sense of the times in which we live. Great composers are no exception, and the Composer's Life *examined Schubert's upbringing and the events of his short, sad life that are so often reflected in his music. The following pages analyze the wider background that inspired and influenced him: the Vienna of the* Biedermeier *period where Schubert made his home and where his friends and patrons lived; and the rapid changes in dress fashions that reflected the increasing pace of historical change that was taking place in the 19th century.*

IN THE BACKGROUND

Changing fashion

Schubert's Vienna

In 1814 the Congress of Vienna met to pacify Europe at the end of the Napoleonic wars. The main aim of the great powers, especially the 'Holy Alliance' of Austria, Prussia and Russia, was to return Europe to the status quo *before 1789 and the outbreak of the French Revolution. The younger brother of the executed Louis XVI was restored to the throne of France as Louis XVIII, and Napoleon's conquests were, where possible, returned to their previous rulers. In this way, the Holy Alliance hoped to stifle the stirrings of democracy amongst their own peoples. For a time, the Austrian Emperor, Francis I, and his Chancellor, Prince Metternich, succeeded in returning Vienna to tranquillity, supported by strict censorship and a network of state spies. Of course, the historical clock could not be turned back – as clearly shown by the rapid changes in 19th-century fashion – and in 1848, the Year of Revolution, the citizens of Vienna rose against imperial oppression.*

IN THE BACKGROUND

'A la mode'

Schubert himself dressed rather scruffily, though his lifetime coincided with a rich succession of new fashions. Some were ludicrous, some sensible, but all testified to the quickening pace of life in the early 19th century.

he beguiling Madame écamier (left) was a elebrated 'pin-up' of ost-revolutionary rance. In her white hemise-dress with its lunging neckline, she xudes all the charm of he empire look from the ip of her neo-Grecian airstyle to her suitably are feet. Her saffron-oloured shawl is raped gracefully on er lap – the wearing of his garment was now an rt in itself.

Schubert's lifetime (1797–1828) coincided with many profound political and economic changes, and, as is often the case, these great changes were reflected in everyday life, particularly in the clothes worn by fashionable people. Then, as until recently, Paris was the unrivalled capital of fashion. Inevitably, the ideals of the French Revolution (1789–99) and the glories of Napoleon's career, which harked back to the austere values of classical civilization, affected what Parisian trend-setters wore. So the great ladies of Napoleon's empire who dressed in simple cotton, or muslin, dresses (known as *robes en chemises*) were consciously reacting against the extravagent styles of Marie-Antoinette's day.

In addition to these political stimuli, there was also an economic basis for the 'empire' look. The increasing activities of England's East India Company in the 17th century had led to the import of fine printed cottons from India. The lightness, colour and variety of this textile made it fashionable among the rich both for dress and furnishings. Bearing in mind that earlier cloths, with the exception of ultra-luxurious silk, had been relatively coarse, heavy and dull, the instant appeal of Indian *calicoes* was not surprising. In the 18th century cotton-growing on a large scale commenced in the southern USA in order to feed the pioneering British cotton 'industry'. (In fact the British cotton industry *was* the early industrial revolution.) With mass production prices came down and then British cotton conquered the world.

Another important factor to account for the vitality of fashion in this period, particularly the speed with which new trends were disseminated, was the invention of the fashion plate in the late 18th century. Published all over Europe, fashion plates enabled ladies and gentlemen in great cities such as Vienna and St Petersburg to copy immediately the very latest *modes de Paris*. Previously, fashionable women had been dependent on access to the mannequin dolls dressed in the latest styles that were laboriously carried about Europe, with an inevitable time-lag, by such enterprising folk as Marie-Antoinette's dressmaker.

The empire look

The white, high-waisted 'empire' gowns with their short, puffed sleeves were so light that it is remarkable that more women did not die of pneumonia, for especially dedicated followers of this influential fashion even dampened them to make them more

lthough children in Schubert's day (right) enefited from a new mphasis on freedom and simplicity, as well as he arrival of cheap and heerful cottons, they were still dressed far more elaborately than children are today. These boys and girls are wearing miniature versions of their parents' clothes.

Mary Evans Picture Library

clinging. Pink or white stockings were often worn beneath as a gesture, and gesture is the word, of modesty, and the necklines were so low that they often revealed more of the bosom than they covered. Madame Hamelin was, like Madame Récamier, a celebrated pioneer of the 'empire' look. She once went to the opera in a dress that exposed her body from one breast to the opposite hip, and she also walked bare-breasted in the Champs Elysées. Although he admired chic women – the Empress Josephine was very stylish – Napoleon tried to restrain the more daring ladies of his court by bricking up fireplaces in the hope that the resulting chill would encourage a degree of modesty.

In their shape dresses continued to be variations on the empire theme until the 1820s. By then significant details had intervened to reduce the purity of the severely classical outfits pioneered by the likes of Madame Récamier and Madame Hamelin. Although the very high waist persisted, dresses began to be tailored to accommodate the bust rather than pushing

Ladies inspect the wares in a textile shop (left). Once the material was purchased and the latest fashion plates were studied, it was up to the ladies themselves or, if they were well-off, their dressmakers, to hand-sew their outfits. The woman below is putting the finishing touches to her satin wedding dress with the help of a maid. The sewing machine was not available until the 1850s.

G. G. Kilburne 'The Wedding Dress'. Phillips, Son & Neale, London/The Bridgeman Art Library

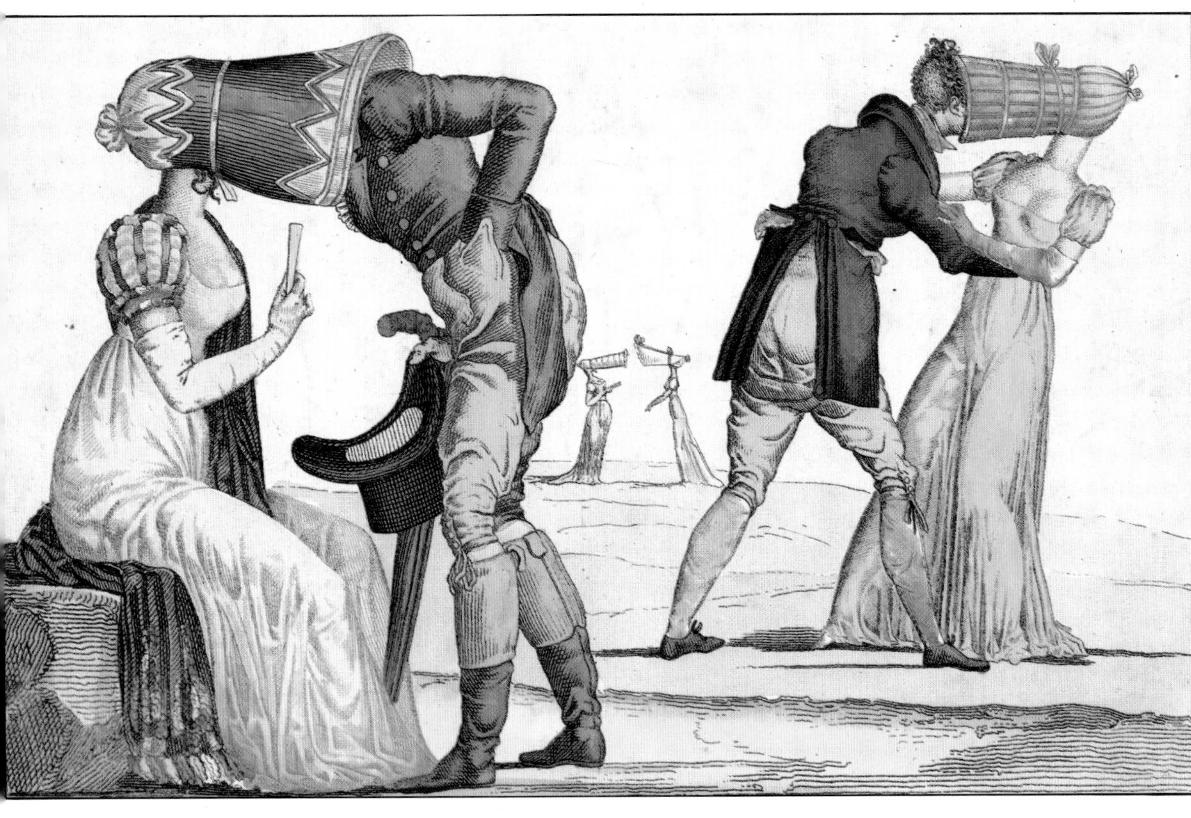

'Les Invisibles en Tête-à-tête'. This French caricature mocks the poke bonnets with exaggeratedly long brims that were in vogue during the 1820s – a period that saw a virtual explosion of millinery styles. Significantly, the men who are here taking advantage of the women's outlandish hats are wearing breeches. Long pantaloons, or trousers, were about to become regulation dress for gentlemen.

it up into an unnaturally high position, and the still floor-length hems began to sprout flounces, embroidery and even ruffs of fur. The little puff sleeves were lengthened and ruffled or pleated, with the leg-o-mutton shape becoming established as a favourite style.

Gradually, too, the fashion for very thin, filmy materials waned and traditionally rich fabrics such as silk, velvet and satin (with coarse printed cottons for the less wealthy) came back into their own, as did colours other than white. Out with the light cottons went the classical-style sandals that went with them and in their place came dainty slippers with low sides and no heel, made of satin or soft leather. The toes were short and rounded and often decorated with a small bow or embroidery. (Needless to say, small feet were admired as a sign of refinement.) In due course, when hems began to rise just a little, these delicate slippers were replaced by shoes and ankle boots.

The arrival of underwear

By the 1820s the traditional feminine shape was re-emerging, as the skirt's width was increased and a greater fullness was introduced at the hips to emphasize the waist. This tendency necessarily required the intervention of that enduring device for female self-exploitation: the corset. This tortuous garment started beneath the bust and ended at the hips. Up until the early 19th century no other underwear, other than petticoats and occasional fads such as the bustle, had been considered necessary – undergarments would, in any case, have ruined the effect of the light chemise dresses. But with the heavier gowns drawers came on the scene. They were usually made of linen, for cotton was considered to be socially inferior for this purpose until later in the 19th century. Drawers were very long and it was considered most indecent to let them be glimpsed beneath the hem of one's dress. Gradually, these pioneering under-garments evolved into relatively tight-fitting pantalettes, fastened just below the knee. Some commentators considered drawers to be indecent and unhealthy and all sorts of tirades were launched against them: 'In high life many women and girls wear drawers, an abominable invention which produces disorders in abundance.' Poor, unfashionable women, however, were spared this abominable invention until much later in the century.

Although considerations of climate had not troubled the wearers of empire gowns unduly because they generally travelled in carriages and lived in comfortable, warm houses, the fashion had nonetheless given rise to all sorts of compensatory outer garments. In one form or another, these outer clothes were destined to stay for a considerable time. Shawls, for example, were now an indispensable item in every woman's wardrobe and wearing one's shawl in a feminine and becoming way was an essential accomplishment. The most prestigious shawls originally came from Kashmir in India but soon Scottish manufacturers were profiting from the successful imitations of them made in Paisley. The pelisse, normally a three-quarter-length coat-gown with raglan, fur-lined sleeves, also made its appearance, as did the pelerine, a cape tied around the shoulders. A version of the male greatcoat known as the redingote, with several overlapping shoulder capes, also arrived to ensure the continued health of fashion-conscious women. A single-breasted jacket from England known as the spencer, which was a small neat-fitting buttoned garment that covered just the bodice of the gown, was also popular.

Accessories and headwear

The fashionable woman paid as much attention to her accessories as she did to the cut of her gowns, for then, as now, they were an all-important element in achieving a total look. At the end of the 18th century mob caps were favoured by day with turbans by night: turbans were often made in the same fabric as the gown and adorned with an ostrich plume. Indeed,

Schubert's lifetime saw an unprecedented cult of headgear, with a virtual explosion of millinery styles in the 1820s. Bonnets of all shapes and sizes were popular, as were straw hats, and they were imaginatively decorated with flowers and ribbons. For hairstyles the empire look had favoured curls. By the 1820s, however, these natural styles had given way to much more complex hairdos, with topknots often elaborated to form bizarre rolls, wings and even horns. Hat-makers had a daunting task designing edifices to sit on these styles.

Gloves and a parasol were important accessories, particularly the latter item, which, when it was not serving as a walking stick, helped to maintain the fair complexion that was the hallmark of gentility. Large fur muffs were also worn and in the evening fans were an all-important female device for communication as much as for ensuring that one glowed gently rather than perspired. One long-term consequence of the chemise-dress was the arrival of the handbag's ancestor in the form of the reticule, or 'ridicule' as it was humorously known. First seen in the 1790s, these small purses served as the pocket which the light chemise-dresses could not sustain. By the 1820s they had diversified into soft leather purses with drawstrings and handbags with flaps and buckles.

Bildarchiv Preussischer Kulturbesitz

BBC Hulton Picture Library

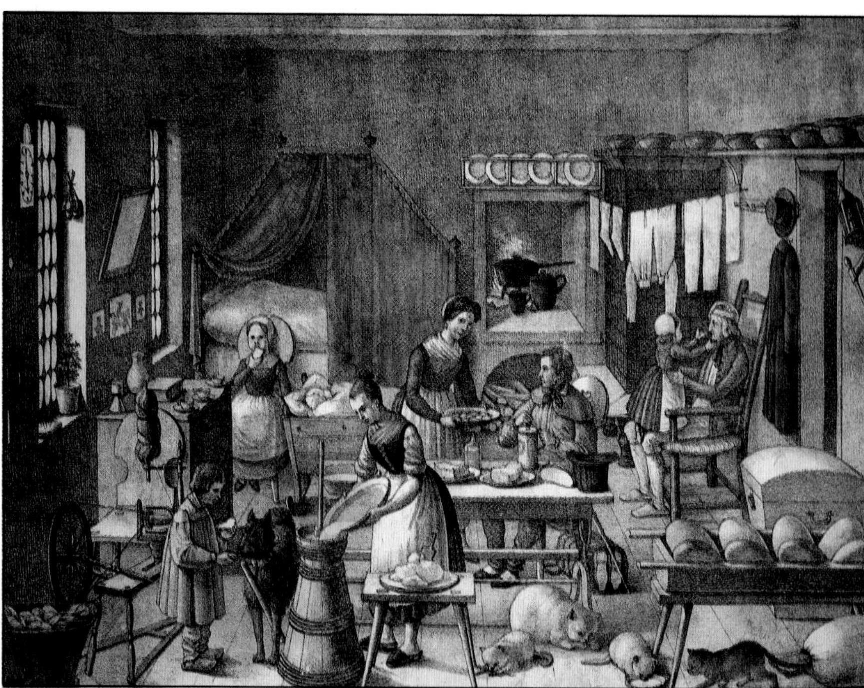

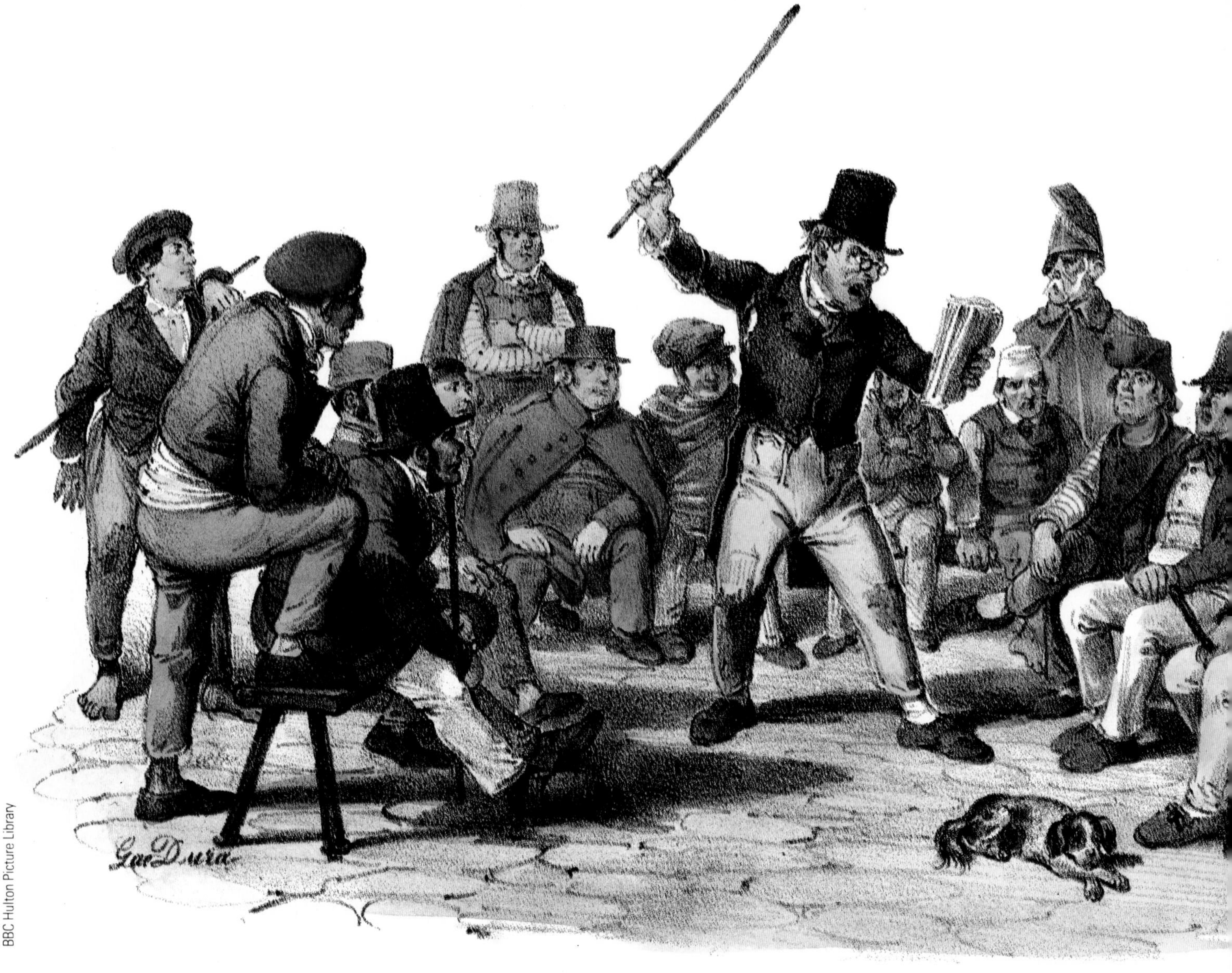

German peasant ousehold (left). The ccupants of this rustic ottage are plainly and ensibly dressed as they o about their daily usiness. The spinning-heel on the left and eir wooden clogs ndicate that, far from ollowing the whims of ashion, their clothes are terally home-spun.

espite their odd hats nd the absence of good hoes, these men (left) re quite fashionable, s almost all of them are lean-shaven and in rousers, while the toryteller in their midst ports a tattered rock-coat and a opper.

The English look

While the ladies of Europe's capitals looked to Paris for the lead in fashion, well-dressed gentlemen were orientated towards England. Just as French ladies had rejected the powdered wigs and stiff satin gowns of the old order in favour of the initially simple empire look, their male counterparts' quest for simplicity took the form of Anglomania. England was seen as the land of liberty and the sombre style of the English country gentleman seemed right for post-revolutionary Europe. Accordingly, wigs, lace ruffles, embroidered coats and silk stockings were abandoned at the end of the 18th century in favour of a smartened 'interpretation' of English country clothes. Schubert's lifetime was in fact the hey-day of the English dandy, whose influential 'king' was George Bryan, or Beau Brummell (1778–1840). The well-dressed Englishman became the ideal man of many a fashionable young lady's dream. Into the head of one of his female heroines the French writer Gautier put this vision:

Sir Edward was so splendidly the Englishman of her dreams. The Englishman freshly shaved, pink, shining, groomed and polished, facing the first rays of the morning sun in an already perfect white cravat . . . Was he not the very crown of civilization?

Until the rise of the dandy even aristocratic male clothes were not designed to fit well, but now the cut and fit of a man's clothes, particularly his jackets and coats, were all-important. The frock-coat, or tail-coat, worn from the time of the French Revolution for both formal or informal wear, ruled the fashionable man until the 1820s. Though styles varied there were, in the main, two quite distinct types: one was cut across at the waist like today's tails and the other was taken at an angle from a very high waist. Both Napoleon and George III adopted this style and with Napoleon in particular a most distinctive profile was created. But there were, of course, many subtle variations on the shape of this basic male 'uniform'.

The waistcoats and breeches that went with these coats were designed to emphasize the waist, and the waistcoat was often laced at the back to facilitate the rather feminine silhouette that was thought desirable. (It is interesting that at a time when fashionable women went around in a state of white near-nudity, their menfolk were relatively colourful and restricted.) The breeches were most often in plain cream, yellow, sage green, or striped, and the waistcoat was in a contrasting colour. Breeches were worn with tight stockings, either plain or patterned, and, for indoor wear, soft black leather pumps decorated with silver buckles, or a small ribbon. Boots served for a gentleman's outdoor footwear.

But the breeches gradually disappeared and then the more trouser-like pantaloons became the universal item of men's dress throughout Europe, notwithstanding considerable variations in cut and length. For daywear they were usually full-length and strapped under the foot like today's ski pants. For evening wear they tended to be a little shorter and were sometimes open-seamed from the calf down and fastened with a row of gold buttons. Pantaloons were sometimes cut loosely over the thigh and then tight from the knee – again emphasizing the feminine silhouette. Over the frock-coat was worn a calf-length cloak for evening, or, for day, the single-breasted great coat with shoulder capes.

Romantic style

Except for a few stubborn oldsters, wigs were dropped by the end of the 18th century, as were queues (pigtails) and manes. Now men's hair was kept fairly short and, for those who fancied themselves as Romantics, it was maintained in a style of rather studied disorder. Although light sideburns were popular, on the whole men were clean-shaven in Schubert's day. By the end of the 18th century the universal three-cornered hat, or tricorne, had been

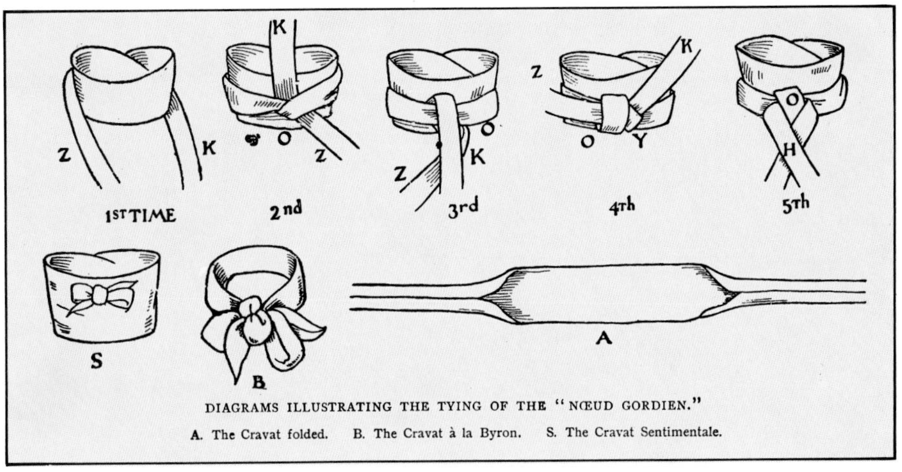

DIAGRAMS ILLUSTRATING THE TYING OF THE "NŒUD GORDIEN."

A. The Cravat folded. B. The Cravat à la Byron. S. The Cravat Sentimentale.

Several key accessories, including a gentleman's cane and a lady's reticule, feature in this 1824 fashion plate (above right). The elegant dandy in the foreground has clearly paid the required attention to his cravat. As men's fashions became more sober such importance was attached to the details of the cravat's many folds (right) that their order was seen as a clue to the wearer's personality and status.

The wealthy Grosvenor family (below) illustrate trends in fashion that were becoming established around the time of Schubert's death (1828). With their very elaborate coiffures – ringlets cascading down the sides of the face were especially popular – and their rich dresses, the Grosvenor women contrast with their more soberly dressed menfolk. From behind, the adult ladies would have presented a back view similar to this detail (right) from a contemporary fashion plate.

Mansell Collection

abandoned in favour of the bicorne, always associate with Napoleon, and an early version of the top hat. B by 1825 the bicorne was passé and the top h evolved so that its sides were parallel and sometim splayed out towards the top. Like wigs, dress swor had all but disappeared by the time of Schubert's bir and in their place came sword sticks, cunning disguised as canes. Tight-fitting gloves becan fashionable in the 1820s, though, unlike those of tl ladies, they were only wrist-length. Other vit accessories included a silver-topped cane and quizzing glass – a small rectangular magnifying glas The lorgnette, a pair of spectacles held by the hand into which they were folded when not in use, was al a popular upper-class accessory from the late 18 century. The art of using a lorgnette was, like the use the fan, a highly complex social game and a tru fashionable gentleman aimed to have all the lorgnett in his vicinity 'turned' upon him.

It is extremely unlikely that Schubert ever carried quizzing glass since he always wore glasses – even bed. But the composer was, like all respectable men his day, at the mercy of his tailor. Indeed, one of th reasons why England was such an important pac setter for men's fashions in the late 18th century w

C. R. Leslie 'The Grosvenor Family'. Fotomas Index

ecause of the expertise of her tailors. Even though :hubert led a busy social life in the coffee houses of ienna and at private gatherings of writers, poets and ·tists, where a certain eccentricity of dress was no oubt tolerated, by 1821 he had incurred debts with oth is tailor and his shoemaker.

But the composer was not unduly concerned with e refinements of up-to-the-minute fashion: he could ot have afforded it. On his death, at the age of nearly 2, he left three cloth coats, three frock-coats, ten airs of pantaloons, nine waistcoats, one hat, five pairs f shoes, two pairs of boots, four shirts, nine eckerchiefs and pocket handkerchiefs and 13 pairs of ocks. For the times and the sort of company that :hubert kept, this was really a very minimal ardrobe. He appears to have had not a little difficulty ith dress since his appearance has been described as at of 'a drunken cabby's'. His great friend, the painter loritz von Schwind, recollected arriving one orning to take Schubert on an excursion: the omposer hurried to finish his dressing and was ummaging in his chest of drawers for a pair of socks. ut, however much he rummaged, every pair turned ut to be hopelessly torn to pieces. 'Schwind', said :hubert at the end of this forlorn inspection, 'Schwind, now I really do believe that whole ones are not knitted any more.'

Gustave Courbet 'The Trout'. Besancon/Bulloz

The mounted peasants in Gustave Courbet's painting of 1855 illustrate the slower pace of changes in dress among ordinary people, especially rural people, in the 19th century. Apart from their hats, they would not have looked very different in the 18th century. But the rather grotesque man with the pig is equipped with an umbrella, an accessory that was not at all common until the end of the century.

The all-important cravat

Most portraits of Schubert show that he wore a neckerchief or cravat in the style of the time, but clearly he did not waste the time upon it that more elegant gentlemen considered necessary. This most important feature of Romantic dress inspired in the year of Schubert's death the publication of *The Art of Tying the Cravat* with its 32 different methods, accompanied by the illustrations of the author, H. Le Blanc. The social implications of how one wore one's cravat were not to be ignored – by the ambitious at any rate:

When a man of rank makes his entrée into a circle distinguished for its taste and elegance, and the usual compliments have passed on both sides, he will discover that his coat will attract only a slight degree of attention, but that the most critical and scrutinising examination will be made on the set *of his Cravat. Should this unfortunately not be correctly and elegantly put on – no further notice will be taken of him; whether his coat be of the reigning fashion or not will be unnoticed by the assembly – all eyes will be occupied in examining the folds of the fatal Cravat.*

His reception will in the future be cold, and no one will move on his entrance, but if his cravat is savamment *and elegantly formed – although his coat may not be of the latest* cut *– every one will rise to receive him with the most distinguished remarks of respect, will cheerfully resign their seats to him, and the delighted eyes of all will be fixed on that part of his person which separates the shoulders from the chin – let him speak downright nonsense, and he will be applauded to the skies; it will be said – 'This man has critically and deeply studied the thirty-two lessons on the Art of Tying the Cravat'.*

That the cravat was such an item of the period and reflected social mores as well as anything else is perhaps summed up by the visitor one morning to the abode of Beau Brummell who found him with his valet

J. Tominc 'Moskonove'. Ljubljana, Narodna Galerija

These assured ladies of the 1830s are partaking of afternoon tea from suitably exquisite porcelain cups – such rituals were integral to refined lifestyles. Despite the continuing popularity of Paisley shawls, the almost sever simplicity of the classic look has now given way to a much more sumptuous style. Note th threesome's positively sculpted hair and their satin dresses, which boast higher necklines, lower waistlines and fashionable leg-o-mutton sleeves.

amid a pile of crumpled cravats. When the visitor enquired, he was told, ruefully, by the valet, 'Sir, those are our failures.'

Children's wear

Upper-class children – boys and girls alike – were usually clothed in dresses of contemporary adult style, until virtually the end of the 18th century. Family portraits abound showing five-year-old boys in waisted, full-skirted dresses and swords, which cannot have afforded them any greater ease of movement than their sisters in their constricting, floor-length dresses. (Boys were usually put in adult-style breeches from about the age of five or six.) Although Schubert was the twelfth child of a poor family, he was nevertheless subject to the rigours of a very formal school uniform. When he was admitted in 1808 at the age of 11 to the Imperial and Royal School his uniform consisted of a brown coat with one epaulette, white breeches, shoes with buckles and a three-cornered hat trimmed with gold braid.

On the subject of children's clothes the great Enlightenment philosopher, Jean-Jacques Rousseau wrote:

The limbs of a growing child should be free to move easily in his clothes; nothing should cramp their growth or movement; there should be nothing tight, nothing fitted closely to the body, no belt of any kind.

By the end of the 18th century, the practice of swaddling babies tightly had died out. Under the new influence of Romanticism, children were often more suitably dressed in lighter, looser clothes.

By Schubert's day fashion had evolved into a symbol of status that was more related to general wealth than to birth, for the French Revolution put an end to aristocratic society as the only 'society': the banker's wife could now successfully vie with the princess. In all ages, however, the dress of peasants and workers has changed less markedly than that of people with leisure and money to indulge in the latest fashion. Many of the ordinary women of Schubert's day, particularly countrywomen, would have been wearing their traditional dirndls, the national dress of the Bavarian and Swiss Alps, with its wide skirt, coloured or white apron, and its distinctive, tight-fitting bodice. Even so, the textile revolution and the great improvements in communication did affect what ordinary folk were wearing in the early 19th century. So although lower-class women wore simple bonnets or caps that were immune to the millinery styles of the big cities, they generally wore simpler, and in summer, cooler clothes than their grandmothers. Their plain skirts and aprons, and their short capes, contrasted with the bulky outfits worn in the 18th century.

All in all, Schubert lived in an age when women's fashion was more simple and less extreme than it had been before his time while for men, a sober and conservative look was adopted which has survived until the last few decades.

IN THE BACKGROUND

'The Biedermeier'

Schubert's cosy and middle-class Vienna concealed a more sinister and repressive one: a police state that tried to stifle creativity and place a tight lid on the city's simmering discontent.

hile the rest of Europe was still recoiling from the iolence of the Napoleonic wars, its old order loodied and shaken, the Viennese were hastily hitewashing over the recent events. Kings had been xecuted, thousands had been slain and Vienna itself ad been occupied by the conquering French, but on after the Congress of Vienna (1815) which edrew the map of Europe, the Viennese middle class ere behaving as though nothing had happened.

Presided over by the clever political manoeuvering f the Austrian Chancellor, Prince Metternich, the ongress tried to write off the French Revolution and to restore the old established values: respect for kingship, material wealth, the social hierarchy and the integrity of the family.

And it was in Vienna itself that this policy was pursued most carefully. Emperor Francis I and his obedient government lulled the Viennese into a gentle slumber, while at the same time, anything which threatened to disrupt the system – such as a free press or student political groups – was subjected to strict censorship, and watched over by an elaborate network of police spies. Out of a period of post-war confidence, and under the machinery of a police state,

One aspect of Vienna was the popular middle-class pastime of promenading through the city's resplendent formal gardens – a far cry from the rigid censorship and police activity that prevailed.

Austria entered the period that came to be known, somewhat insultingly, as 'Biedermeier'.

Biedermeier

This word was coined around 1850 as Austria was becoming industrialized and entering the modern world. People looked back on the period after 1815 as a time of sleepy domesticity and 'Biedermeier' became their condescending label for that epoch. Biedermeier was made up from the German adjective 'bieder' meaning plain or inoffensive, and Meier – one of the commonest German surnames. (The English equivalent might be 'the style of the conservative and rather boring Mr. Smith'.)

At first, Biedermeier was a mocking reference to the domesticated and dull cultural life of Austria between the Congress of Vienna in 1815, and the revolution that finally shattered the tranquillity of Vienna in 1848. But later, people came to admire the simple style and décor and the humane quality of family life at this time: Biedermeier became a general term to describe Austrian culture during that time – particularly the style of Vienna.

Archiv für Kunst und Geschichte

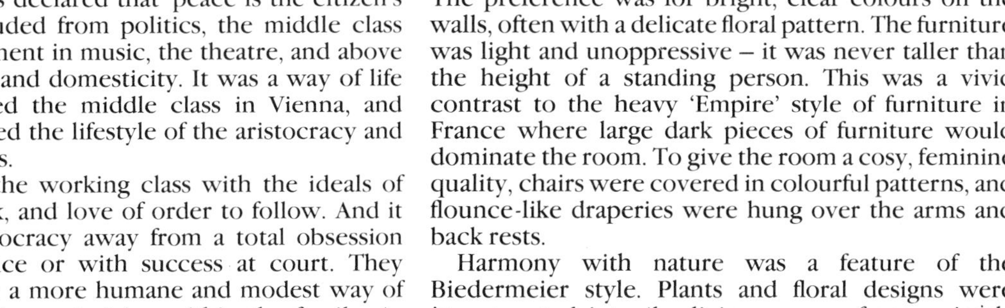

e living-rooms of the ll-to-do during the riod known as edermeier (1815–48) were comfortably corated with parquet ors, clear colours and host of ornaments ft).

ousehold typical of e time (below left): a rge musically inclined mily steeped in mesticity.

e preoccupation of the ennese with the family it and the display of ancial security is phasized in this inting by Waldmüller elow) – during this riod the best known of enna's artists.

In 1815 it was declared that 'peace is the citizen's first duty'. Excluded from politics, the middle class looked for fulfilment in music, the theatre, and above all in family life and domesticity. It was a way of life which dominated the middle class in Vienna, and which also shaped the lifestyle of the aristocracy and the working class.

It presented the working class with the ideals of thrift, hard work, and love of order to follow. And it turned the aristocracy away from a total obsession with extravagance or with success at court. They began to pursue a more humane and modest way of life, seeking their greatest joy within the family. As Adalbert Stifter, Austria's greatest novelist of the time expressed it: 'pure family life is our greatest happiness, a happiness which appears inexhaustible.' But it was above all in the style of the middle-class home that Biedermeier values were seen most clearly.

The home and music

The living-room became the focal point of the home: it was a room to be lived in and enjoyed by the whole family. All trace of pomp and formality was banished.

The preference was for bright, clear colours on the walls, often with a delicate floral pattern. The furniture was light and unoppressive – it was never taller than the height of a standing person. This was a vivid contrast to the heavy 'Empire' style of furniture in France where large dark pieces of furniture would dominate the room. To give the room a cosy, feminine quality, chairs were covered in colourful patterns, and flounce-like draperies were hung over the arms and back rests.

Harmony with nature was a feature of the Biedermeier style. Plants and floral designs were incorporated into the living-room – from a simple stand for a potted plant to elaborate *jardinières* which included goldfish bowls and bird cages. The conservatory became a customary feature of middle-class homes, so that nature could be enjoyed during the winter. Around April it was common for the better-off families to rent a villa in the beautiful wooded suburbs of Vienna for the spring and summer months.

The dining-room was the next most important room, dominated by a large expandable dining-table, surrounded by chairs. The sideboard was becoming a common piece of furniture and stood along one wall. The larger houses also had a study for the master of the house, and a dressing room for the lady as well as a bedroom for the parents, rooms for the children, and accommodation for the servants. But within the living-room there was often a special working area for the housewife, containing a small sewing table and a seat. More well-to-do households would have a music corner in the living-room, with instruments that suited the talents of the family, as making music together would be one of the principal joys of the typical Biedermeier household.

In the musical circle that surrounded Schubert we can see a specially gifted group of young people, but engaged in music in a way that was typical of the Biedermeier household. At first, Schubert's father and his three sons played together as a string quartet. As the group expanded, they moved to the house of a friendly merchant, and then to the home of a violinist friend, Otto Hatwig, who became the leader of the orchestra.

Memoirs from this time record music groups in the homes of a university professor, a general, senior civil servants, a brewer, a calligrapher, wholesale merchants and retail traders. Both Schubert and the greatest poet of this period, Franz Grillparzer, attended the musical soirées of the banker Johann von Geymüller. Legend has it that Geymüller's home contained five pianos: one for each of his exceptionally musical daughters.

Schubert set some of Grillparzer's poems to music and both were bewitched by the intelligent and spirited singing of these sisters. When one of this lively and constantly changing group was particularly struck by a song 'our Schubert' had written, he would make a copy and show it to friends, or send it to Salzburg or Munich. Through these informal musical groups, Schubert's work circulated around Vienna and Austria; Schubert himself was never over-concerned about getting his work published.

Painting

Painting in Austria at this time provides an interesting mirror reflecting the values of Biedermeier society. While artists in France, Germany, and England were being drawn towards the themes of nature that had a violent, transcendental quality, the painters of Vienna

Staatliche Museen Preussischer Kulturbesitz, Berlin

concentrated on family life and on flowers.

In England, Turner was painting landscapes whe the light battered the viewer like a physical force. Germany, Casper Friedrich was creating alpine vie that had the intensity of a religious vision. But Austria, landscape painting remained picturesque a precise and never hurled itself into the Romant abyss. Instead, the themes that came to epitomi Vienna during its Biedermeier phase – bourge simplicity in place of aristocratic pomp, the co home in place of the palace, the lovable details everyday life in place of the big moments of historic conflict – found an apt form of expression in the wor of the typical exponents of Austrian art.

The greatest artist of this time, Ferdinand Geo Waldmüller, developed his own style of lumino intensity to paint both landscapes of great clarity, a simple paintings of family groups where the figur harmonized with their background in a way that w both elegant and natural.

But though Waldmüller's art is now acclaimed totally characteristic of Biedermeier Vienna, in h own life he fought a series of tedious and ultimate dangerous battles with the artistic establishment. H did not fit in either with the classically inspir painters, or with the Nazarenes (the German versi of the pre-Raphaelites). Instead, he argued agair 'chewing the cut of things handed down' and becau of this critical attitude towards tradition he w relieved of his teaching job at the Academy of Fi Arts in Vienna.

Instead, Waldmüller obtained a job as a curator o gallery, but was pensioned off after writing memorandum on reforms needed in the teaching art: he had not sent his criticisms through the corre channels. By the time that he died, Waldmüller's wo fetched no price at all. His life is a good example of t Viennese tradition of stifling talent and ultimat ignoring it.

Theatre

The world of theatre also tells us how people w were tormented and even destroyed by the attitu of their time, were later remembered as personifyi

In his choice of subject-matter the Viennese artist von Engert epitomized the spirit of homeliness: an enclosed flower garden with a vine pergola, hollyhocks and sunflowers (above). Among these suburban images a woman sits knitting and reads what is almost certainly a Bible.

Staatliche Museen Preussischer Kulturbesitz, Berlin

Outside Vienna, painters like Caspar David Friedrich scorned the pedestrian Biedermeier style and chose a totally different mood and subject. The sense of the infinite is hauntingly portrayed in Friedrich's **Moon rising over the Sea** ***(right).***

all the things that Vienna symbolizes: romance, gaiety, and a love of life.

Ferdinand Raimund was the greatest dramatic figure of the period. He was stage-struck at the age of 13 and worked his way up through a troupe of travelling players, until, by the age of 18, he had begun to establish himself on the Viennese stage as a new kind of comedian: one who could be both subtle and gentle. Raimund fell in love with Toni, daughter of a coffee house proprieter, but her parents were too snobbishly middle-class to accept an actor as a son-in-law. Against the wishes of their daughter, they rejected Raimund's suit. In despair, he had a brief flirtation with an actress who happened to be the daughter of his director and patron, who forced him to marry the girl. Raimund was now in double trouble. He had to obtain a divorce from a wife he did not love, and somehow retain the affection of his beloved Toni and win the approval of her parents. Surprisingly, Raimund was also a deeply religious Catholic, and after obtaining his divorce he did not feel himself free to re-marry. Instead, over a small shrine in a vineyard in the Vienna Woods, he and Toni swore a vow before God to be true to each other.

While enduring such a complicated and unhappy private life, Raimund wrote a series of plays that made him the comic genius of his time. Yet beneath the social satire there was a sad and haunting perception of life passing people by. In his most famous work – *Das Mädchen aus der Feenwelt oder Der Bauer als Millionär* ('The Girl from Fairyland or the Peasant Turned Millionaire') – Raimund himself played a simple peasant, Fortunatus Wurzel, who in a flash is transformed on stage from a vigorous youth into a bent and almost senile 'Aschenmann', a dustman who collects wood ash while singing a sad little song with a chorus: 'All is ashes, all is ashes.'

After nine years of painful devotion to his beloved Toni, the girl's parents finally relented and allowed the couple to live together in their home. But this torment had taken its toll of Raimund's spirit. In 1836 he was bitten by a dog, and for some reason Vienna's greatest comic genius convinced himself that the dog was rabid and he was about to contract the disease, so he

Bildarchiv Preussischer Kulturbesitz

For the Viennese middle class, going to the theatre was a chance to parade their prosperity (left). But beneath this opulent veneer lay a sense of stagnation and time passing by which was cleverly satirized by Vienna's most popular actor, Ferdinand Raimund (above with actress Constanze Dahn).

Venice, Correr Museum/Salmer

Reproduced by gracious permission of Her Majesty The Queen

Emperor Francis I (above) and his Chancellor, Prince Metternich (above right) collaborated on a policy that diverted attention away from Europe's political ferment. Although Vienna seemed free of unrest it was at a price – in 1801 the Austrian Ministry of Police took over the administration of censorship.

picked up a gun and committed suicide.

The theatre provided a rich source of interest and gossip for Vienna, and the Austrian police recognized the value of the theatre during periods of public tension. When closure of the theatres was suggested, the Police Department replied: 'People are accustomed to theatrical shows. In times like these, when individuals are affected by so much suffering, the police are more than ever obliged to cooperate in the diversion of citizens by every moral means. The most dangerous hours of the day are the evening hours. They cannot be filled more innocently than in the theatre.'

The theatre was not just for the wealthy or the middle class. It also faithfully reflected the attitudes of working class and petit bourgeois audiences, and enjoyed the loyalty of all Vienna. In 1813, a fortnight after an army commanded by the Austrian Prince Schwarzenberg defeated Napoleon at Leipzig, a new hit appeared on the Vienna stage, written by a clever young journalist Adolf Bäuerle. It was *Die Burger in Wien* ('Citizens of Vienna') and the character who made the play a sensational success was Staberl: a whining embodiment of the 'little man'; an umbrella maker; a buffoon; the despair of his friends; and yet one of life's survivors. All of his speeches and complaints ended despairingly 'I wish it did me some good . . .'.

It was an apt 'catch' phrase for a nation that had been defeated by Napoleon, allied to Napoleon through marriage, and had finally vanquished Napoleon. A nation which was told by a benevolent dictator of an emperor not to worry about politics, and to concentrate on domestic life. 'I wish it did me some good . . .' was the cry of Vienna's man in the street every time he got entangled in some wild idea that went wrong.

The police state

The price to be paid for all this domestic bliss was nothing less than a highly organized police state. Metternich knew that what he was trying to keep out of Austria was the *Zeitgeist* or 'spirit of the age'. Nationalism, the Romantic Movement, talk of revolutionary political ideas, were all sweeping across Europe, and for Metternich censorship and a well organized police system were the best defence.

To keep the universities as quiet as possible, Metternich and his ministers reformed th curriculum. Controversial areas such as philosoph were allowed to rot, while the study of science an technology was encouraged. 'Anyone can philosophi and criticize as the spirit moves him, but positiv science must be learned,' as Metternich's chief aic Friedrich von Gentz put it. Any university lectur teaching the doctrine of free thought was relieved his job. Any student suspected of belonging to political association could be put under detention an deported to the provinces. These policies were success for Metternich and the universities remaine quiet. Meanwhile, an elaborate network of polic informers watched over the people of Vienna.

When Schubert died in poverty in 1828, th circumstances of his burial bore some resemblance t Mozart's, who was buried in a pauper's grave. On interesting difference was a sentence in the municip report which asked 'Whether there were books amor the property of the deceased and whether a repo about them had been made to the Imperial Boc Revision Office'. This was standardized procedure fc uncovering any subversive pamphlets that might h

F. G. Waldmüller 'Children eating their breakfast', Nationalgalerie, Prague

mong the deceased person's possessions. In 1830 the ystem was further tightened up because revolution ad driven the French king from his throne, and hreatened to contaminate Austria.

An unsuccessful attempt was made to halt the flood f people from the countryside into the city. From the rench experience it was realized that a mobile orking class was the most likely group to cause olitical trouble and the word 'proletariat' was nported from France to describe this new and angerous social force.

Emperor Francis I passed laws to restrict the uilding of new houses. Casual workers had to obtain pecial marriage permits from the police in an attempt o prevent the working class from reproducing too apidly, and for a time a complete ban was placed on ew factories being established in Vienna.

he City

ienna had grown to embrace a population of 326,000 eople by 1830. About a quarter of these lived in the entre still surrounded by the medieval walls of the ity. The rest lived in the suburbs which increased rapidly despite Imperial attempts to keep the lid on the population.

Such rapid growth, unsupported by any major building programme, did not produce a healthy environment. Schubert died in 1828 of typhus at the age of 31, the same disease that had killed his mother. Typhus, dysentery, and tuberculosis were rife in the city, and the infant mortality rate was high.

Schubert's father had fourteen children from his first two marriages – only five children survived. His brother Ferdinand married twice and had 25 children – only 12 survived. In 1831 half the Viennese who died were under 20 years old. In real terms, the population of the city was actually falling because of the high death rate. It was only the constant arrival of new workers from the Austrian Empire which made Vienna appear to grow in population.

Evidence from the courts and from police records shows that there was real misery bordering on starvation for the working class. And corruption was common among the poorly paid lower clerks of the public services, as they tried to supplement their meagre wages with bribes.

Student uprisings (below) were the inevitable reaction to a repressive regime, though in Vienna they never attracted the same fanatical support given to the other similar demonstrations that were taking place throughout Europe.

Österreichisches Nationalbibliothek

Not far from Vienna's glorious palaces there were ramshackle streets peopled by the city's destitute (left). Such poverty was not, of course, peculiar to Vienna, but in a city where complacency ruled it seemed more of a disgrace.

Since the published word was strictly censored few had the courage to speak out against the establishment. However, the poet Grillparzer (right) was a notable exception.

Bildarchiv Preussischer Kulturbesitz

When unskilled workers in a village near Vienna went on strike, their leaders were sentenced to hard labour in chains. When bakers' shops were looted during the bread riots in 1805 the cavalry were required to clear the streets, leaving ten dead behind them. In 1811, over 1500 shoemakers demonstrated in Vienna until military strength dispersed the march. Even as conditions improved after the war, a quick rise in the price of some basic item such as candles was enough to trigger off a dangerous state of unrest in the poorer quarters.

Although the official message of the Biedermeier period was that 'happiness in a quiet corner' was the best policy for the good citizen to follow, numerous accounts tell us how aware people were of their extremely limited freedom: freedom which amounted to being able to sit at home, think of nothing much and enjoy a quiet life.

The French

The poet Grillparzer was a patriotic youth who took part in the defence of Vienna against Napoleon's bombardment in 1809. But while the French were actually occupying the city, they were hardly regarded as a hated invading army. If anything, they inspired admiration. The French officers with their experience of revolution, their military success, their political sophistication, seemed to come from a world very different from the humdrum and quiet life of Vienna. The poet Grillparzer tells us how obsessed he became by Napoleon at this time:

I myself was no less an enemy of the French than m father, and yet Napoleon fascinated me with a mag power. I had hatred in my heart; I had never been addicted to military displays, and yet I missed not one of his reviews of troops. I still see him before m running rather than walking down the steps of Schönbrunn [the huge palace on the outskirts of Vienna] and then standing there like cast-iron to survey his troops on the march past with the unmoved look of the lord and master. He put me under a spell as a snake does a bird. My father mus have been little pleased by these unpatriotic excursions but he never forbade me.

Napoleon was finally defeated and for 15 years t Viennese lived in a state of apparent Biedermei tranquillity. But in 1830 two years after Schuber death, disturbing news reached them of anoth revolution in France. Once again the French h shown what being in control of your own politic destiny could mean.

In his Journal Grillparzer wrote:

The French have driven out their king who tried to break the constitution and turn them into a variet of Austrian, which civically and politically, seems t be the worst fate that could happen to anyone. I wis I were in France. It is still better to live in the dang of democracy than to have the spirit defeated and th noblest human needs sacrificed to an abominable system of stability.

Most Viennese looked on in amazement at the revolutionary enthusiasm of the French. But there was also a degree of admiration and envy when, in 1830, the Parisians rebelled yet again (below) and drove out their king.

Carnavalet/Giraudon

THE GREAT COMPOSERS

Fryderyk Chopin

1810-1849

Chopin's image – that of the passionate and consumptive Romantic, exiled from, but longing for, his native land, pouring forth his heart in impassioned outbursts of piano music – has obscured the fact that his music has none of the expected trappings of Romanticism. In everything he wrote there is a Classic purity and discretion and not a sign of Romantic exhibitionism. Unlike Liszt, his flamboyant contemporary, Chopin gave few public recitals, preferring to earn his living through private teaching or playing for small, select groups. Yet the tragic story of Poland, the country he left at the age of 20, never to revisit, constantly informed his art. His polonaises and mazurkas transformed the primitive rhythms and melodies he had heard in his youth into enduring art forms. The influence of the great Italian singers of his age taught him the art of 'singing' on the piano, most evident in his nocturnes. Though his total output was small and almost limited to solo piano music, its range is vast, fully justifying his legendary reputation.

Chopin had left Poland for Vienna in 1830 when he heard of the national uprising which was soon to be brutally crushed. This decided him never to return and in 1831, having had no luck in Vienna, he moved to Paris. Here he found fame, inspiration and love – in the person of George Sand. He also found, in the circle of Romantics such as Berlioz, Liszt and Delacroix, welcoming kindred spirits. For Paris, as In the Background *shows, was then the cultural capital of Europe, and the 1830s was the high tide of French Romanticism. Paris, as the following pages relate, became Chopin's second home, and there he died. His style, however, remained distinctively his own. The Etude in C minor, the famous 'Revolutionary' etude, was inspired by news of the Polish rising and written in 1831, before he reached Paris, yet it shows already his essential style in one aspect. Another side of his genius appears in the Nocturne in E flat, written in 1830. Both works are analyzed in* Listener's Guide.

COMPOSER'S LIFE

'Crowds petrify me'

Behind the dazzling virtuoso and inspired composer lay another Chopin – a patriotic Pole, a tormented lover, a man who was terrified by large audiences and one who was racked by a terrible illness.

Archiv für Kunst und Geschichte

'hopin at the age of 19 – nd by now recognized s a national composer playing before 'istinguished guests in e salon of Prince 'adziwill in Berlin. adziwill, himself a ellist and tenor, took a een interest in Chopin's areer.

More than that of any other composer, the name of Chopin has become associated with one instrument – the pianoforte. At a time when Europe was well provided with keyboard virtuosi, Thalberg, Kalkbrenner, Moscheles and Liszt among them, Chopin's reputation was widely considered to stand above them all, despite the fact that he had no love for the concert platform and in his whole lifetime gave scarcely 30 public performances.

Although Poland at the time of Chopin's birth was enjoying a period of comparative calm in terms of its political struggles with Russia, national pride was strong, and in his music Chopin forged a spiritual link with his country and its people that distance and years of exile could never destroy. The national identity asserts itself not only in the pieces based on Polish dance forms (the polonaises and mazurkas), but in the use of elements from Polish folk music and in the pervasive strain of melancholy that seem to linger beneath the surface even in the most serene passages of his work.

Chopin's letters to his Polish friends reveal a lively intelligence and ever-present sense of humour. His accounts of the musical and social occasions he attended are incisive and witty; but though he was quick to scorn social and musical pretentiousness of all kinds in private correspondence, his behaviour was always kind, courteous and infinitely considerate. No one, having met Chopin, could fail to like him, and it is interesting to note how many of his pupils became staunch companions and helpers in later life when his own physical powers were fading. His foibles, such as his indecisiveness in matters great and small (whether to leave Poland, which jacket to wear for a concert),

Photo Harlingue-Viollet

Chopin's parents, Justyna and Nicolas (above) were married in 1806. They settled down in a house on the Zelazowa Wola Estate (below) near Warsaw, and it was here that Chopin was born four years later.

seemed trivial in the light of his other traits, for he was a constant friend, an affectionate son and brother, a sympathetic colleague and a generous, patient teacher.

Early evidence of genius

Fryderyk Franciszek Chopin was born at Zelazowa Wola, near Warsaw, on either 1 March 1810 (as Chopin himself believed) or, as his certificate of baptism states, probably erroneously, 22 February 1810. The 1 March date is now generally accepted. His father was Nicolas Chopin, born in Marainville, Vosges, in 1771. As a young man, Nicolas had left Franch to seek his fortune, served in the Polis National Guard, became a tutor of French in Polis aristocratic circles and, in 1810, was appointed as teacher of French at the Warsaw Lyceum; soon afte he took a part-time post teaching French at th Military School as well. He had married Justyn Krzyzanowska (born 1782) in June 1806. Thei daughter Ludwika had been born in 1807, and Isabell (1811) and Emilia (1813) were soon to follow.

Fryderyk's childhood, despite the recent politica upheavals in Poland, was a secure and happy one. Th family moved from Zelazowa Wola to Warsaw i October 1810 so that Nicolas could take up hi Lyceum post and were allotted a large apartment i the former Saxon Palace which also housed th school. Justyna was able to supplement Nicolas's smal income by taking in boarders, some of whom becam Fryderyk's most devoted friends.

From his earliest years Fryderyk showed a pre cocious gift for music – he was playing duets with hi elder sister Ludwika before he had had any forma training – and also for drawing caricatures, writin verses and, with his sisters, devising comedies whic they performed to celebrate family anniversarie When he was six, Fryderyk began taking lessons from local piano teacher, Wojciech Zywny, an eccentri 60-year-old Czech. A violinist by training, compose and occasional conductor, Zywny channelled Fryderyk' outstanding natural ability, both physical and inter pretative, into the German classical repertoire – Bac Haydn, Mozart and Beethoven – as well as guiding hi through pieces by popular contemporary composer such as Hummel, an early influence on Chopin's ow compositions, and the great virtuoso Kalkbrenner.

Fryderyk constantly improvised pieces of his ow

Barnabys Picture Library

ıich, at first, Zywny would note down for him. A ›lonaise in G minor was published in 1817, and the arsaw press commented with pride on the child's ›hievements, both pianistic and creative: 'Geniuses : born in our country also, but the lack of publicity les them from the public.' Fryderyk's fame spread ›t, and local ladies showered him with invitations to ay at their homes. Hailed as a second Mozart, he gave › first public performance at the Radziwill Palace in ›18, aged eight, playing a piano concerto by rowetz. In 1821 Fryderyk wrote a farewell lonaise for Zywny, who admitted that there was ›thing more he could teach the boy, and soon began ‹ing composition lessons from Jósef Elsner, director the new Warsaw Conservatoire.

In the summer holidays Fryderyk, always physically il, was sent to the village of Szafarnia for country air, ›d and exercise. Here he heard traditional Polish k-music – a lifelong influence – and sketched some his first mazurkas. After three years at the Lyceum 823–26), Fryderyk enrolled at the Conservatoire. › Opus 1, a Rondo in C minor, was published in June 25, and his public performances while a student :luded demonstrations on the aelopantaleon and lomelodicon (hybrid organ/piano instruments). ar Alexander I gave him a diamond ring after hearing n perform on the latter.

As a student, and ever after, Fryderyk avidly attend as many musical evenings, concerts and operas as could. He admired Rossini's *Barber of Seville* and eber's *Der Freischütz,* but even though he had never ard a first-rate company he realized that perforances by the Polish National Opera left much to be sired. In 1828, after seeing *Der Freischütz,* he ›served: 'The choir kept missing their cues and coming in a quarter beat behind each other.' It would not be long before he felt the need to go abroad in search of wider, more enriching musical experience. Meanwhile, under Elsner's sympathetic eye, he continued composing for the piano. Attempts to conform to classical structures were less successful as were his efforts at orchestration, in which Elsner always encouraged him. But works such as the flamboyant *Là ci darem* variations, op. 2, which exploited his own gifts as a pianist, revealed how fast he was moving towards his mature style. His distinctively fluent and flexible treatment of melody and elegant use of keyboard configurations were already much in evidence.

An opportunity to visit Berlin arose, giving Fryderyk a chance to widen his musical horizons, yet although he found himself present at the same function as Zelter, Spontini and Mendelssohn (only a year older than Chopin, but already a prolific and widely acclaimed composer) he lacked the courage to speak to them. A year later, in 1829, he managed to get to Vienna to supervise publication of some early works, and on 11 August made his true professional début at the Kärtnertortheater, where his performance of his *Krakowiak,* op. 14, and op. 2 Variations, both with orchestra, had a tumultuous reception. Even better received, however, was his improvisation on a Polish drinking-song. A second concert followed a week later,

A view of Warsaw (left) around the time of Chopin's boyhood. At the age of eight, he gave his first concert here at a charity fête in the Radziwill Palace.

His feet well clear of the pedals and his face set in concentration, the young Chopin entertains his friends with his precocious piano playing (below).

By courtesy of the Trustees of the Tate Gallery, London

As an adolescent, Chopin (right), when he was not composing, tried his hand at caricatures. Above is one of a Polish peasant as seen through the young composer's eyes.

and then, fired with his success, he returned to Warsaw determined to find a way of establishing his reputation outside Poland. His last year (as it turned out) in his native land was marked by a series of largely abortive plans to tour abroad, his love for a young mezzo-soprano, Konstancia Gladkowska (a student at the Conservatoire) and the composition of his two piano concertos – the first of which (no. 2 in F minor) had a slow movement inspired by his passion for Konstancia.

Chopin leaves Poland

On 11 November 1830, Chopin left Poland – initially for Vienna, but stopping en route at Dresden where he improvised for the Court. This time, however, Vienna was less interested in the young Polish genius; during eight frustrating months there he gave only two performances (4 April, 11 June), neither of which had anything like the impact of his earlier concerts. Otherwise he spent this time hearing as much music as possible, including opera, and in completing an impressive body of work: mazurkas, waltzes (including the Grande Valse Brillante, op. 18 in E flat), his B minor Scherzo and his last orchestrated work, the Grande Polonaise in E flat. He also sketched out his first ballade (G minor).

When he left Vienna, it was for 'London, via Paris', according to his passport: years afterwards he would jokingly remind his Paris friends that he was just

When Chopin arrived in Paris in mid-September 1831, he discovered a city of quaint gentility (right). But a few months later, in February 1832, he was whisked into the glitter of Parisian high life when he gave his first and much-acclaimed Paris concert.

ıssing through. En route in Stuttgart he heard that a ·w Polish revolt had been bloodily suppressed by the ıssians, and that Warsaw was in Russian hands. His ·ief for his homeland overwhelmed him, and it has ten been suggested that the news could have inspired s turbulent Etude op. 10 no. 12 ('Revolutionary').

A week later in Paris (September 1831) Chopin took ·dgings at 27 Blvd Poissonière. The city had become ıe political refugee club for half Europe as well as a ecca for artists of all types and nationalities. Through 's compatriots – the only people with whom he could el completely at ease – Chopin came to meet leading gures of the Romantic movement, while Liszt, Mendelohn, Osborne and Hiller – all pianists – and the cellist ·anchomme became his closest musical associates.

Despite being part of such an influential circle, it ·as five months before he made his Paris début, at the ılle Pleyel on 26 February 1832. There he played, ithout orchestra, the F minor Concerto and *Là ci ırem* variations, as well as taking part in a 6-piano ‹travaganza by Kalkbrenner. For Chopin the concert ·as an artistic triumph. The critic Fétis wrote: 'an ›undance of original ideas, . . . His inspiration paves ıe way for a fundamental change of form [in piano ›mpositions]'. The performance was not a financial ıccess, however. Money was a problem, despite the ct that he had acquired a few pupils from the Polish ›mmunity, and Chopin described himself at this time

Roger-Viollet

Carnavalet/Bulloz

as suffering from 'consumption of the purse'. Soon, however, with his appearance at a Rothschild soirée, matters improved dramatically: now that his reputation as a brilliant musician was acknowledged in fashionable society, he became the most sought-after piano teacher in Paris. Mme de Rothschild herself was one of his pupils.

By 1832 he was said to be the lover of the rich and musically talented countess Delfina Potocka, who was separated from her husband. Chopin dedicated to her the F minor Concerto that Konstancia Gladkowska (now married) had partly inspired two years earlier. (Much later he would also dedicate to Delfina his Waltz op. 64 no. 1, the so-called 'Minute Waltz'.) He found it easier to work, however, when Delfina was not in Paris to consume his time and his emotions. At the time his Etudes op. 25 were his main concern, but he was also writing nocturnes and mazurkas, completing work on his G minor Ballade and sketching out some preludes. Liszt had been playing some of his études, to the composer's wholehearted approval: 'I wish I could steal from him his manner of playing my études', he remarked to Ferdinand Hiller in a letter dated 20 June 1833.

The concerts in which Chopin participated that year (he was not the principal performer) did nothing to further his career; his 1834 performances were likewise few and insignificant, and 1835 saw two performances, in April (4 and 26) which confirmed Chopin's aversion to playing in public concerts: the first, which included the Paris première of his E minor Concerto, was damned with faint praise, and although the second, featuring his Andante spianato and Grand Polonaise in E flat (op. 22), was far better received, the hurt of the earlier experience was not forgotten.

Chopin had neither the temperament nor the physical constitution for the life of a concert pianist. He suffered agonies before public concerts:

I wasn't meant to play in public... Crowds intimidate me, their breath stifles me, their stares petrify me, their strange faces throw me into

The drawing-room of Chopin's apartment in Square D'Orléans (above) where he moved in 1842. George Sand lived next-door-but-one and she wrote, 'we are for ever running in and out of each other's houses at night.'

As a student and later when in Paris, Chopin was strongly influenced by Rossini's* Barber of Seville, *for which the costume (below) was designed.

Lauros-Giraudon

Archiv für Kunst und Geschichte

When Chopin stopped in Dresden (right) in 1825, he intended to renew a boyhood friendship with the son of the Wodzińska family. Instead, he began a courtship with the 16-year old Maria (above) which soon became a passionate – though short-lived – love affair.

Collection Viollet

confusion. But it's different for you: if you can't captivate them, you dominate them.

That summer Chopin travelled – first to Carlsbad t meet his parents, for the last time, then to Dresde where he fell in love with the 16-year-old Mari Wodzińska. He wanted to marry her, but the matc was not encouraged by her parents and the romanc was eventually to peter out. From Dresden he went t Leipzig to meet Mendelssohn, who introduced him t the young Clara Wieck – at 15 already established as concert pianist. It was at her home that Chopin firs met Robert Schumann, the man who had honoure him in 1830 with the famous exclamation: 'Hats of gentlemen, a genius!' The two were never close Chopin was embarrassed by the fulsome praise Schu mann lavished on him in reviews: 'He exaggerates s much he makes me look ridiculous.' As he did no much admire Schumann's music, he could not retur the compliment, either, though he did dedicate hi second ballade to him (op. 38). Clara's interpretatio of his own work was another matter: Chopin was mos favourably impressed.

Affair with George Sand

In October 1836, at the home of Liszt and his mistress Countess Marie D'Agoult, Chopin was introduced t the prolific novelist George Sand (Aurore Dudevant) He was not instantly attracted to her ('I did not like he face . . . There is something off-putting about her') George Sand was fascinated by genius of all kinds however, and musical enough to want to share i Chopin's creative life in some way. She invited hin

George Sand's drawing-room in the secret love-nest at Nohant (left) in the heart of France. Here, in the warm climate, that suited his ever-precarious health, Chopin wrote many of his finest pieces and enjoyed a satisfying domestic life with George Sand.

often to meet her circle of friends – Alfred de Musset, Heine, the Polish poet Mickiewicz and the artist Delacroix, among many others. While he resisted the convention-flouting siren – who not only smoked cigars and wore men's clothes in public but also was none too discreet about her many lovers – she began to experience a deep longing for Chopin.

The following summer he refused her invitation to join her and several of his compatriots at her country house in Nohant. Indeed, most unexpectedly, but perhaps because of his depression after the breaking of his engagement to Maria Wodzińska, he left with his friend Camille Pleyel for a two-week visit to London. Here he maintained the lowest profile possible: he played only once, at the house of the piano manufacturer James Broadwood, where he was introduced as M. Fritz. A mere bar or two of his playing was, however, enough to reveal conclusively his true identity.

In the summer of 1838 Chopin at last yielded to George Sand's love – a selfless devotion fired not only by passion but by her desire for a family life (she had two children, Maurice and Solange, by her husband Casimir Dudevant). Always discreet about their liaison, they decided to spend their first winter together in Majorca, where, they had assumed, the climate would have a beneficial effect on Chopin's health. At first, when they arrived on 8 November, the Mediterranean landscape, day-long sunshine and relaxed atmosphere combined to give Chopin a feeling of well-being and he embarked upon several new compositions. But with the arrival of the damp and windy winter weather his tubercular symptoms reappeared. He had been very ill in 1835, and the *Warsaw Courier* had issued a denial of his death in 1836; now, once again, he was coughing violently and spitting blood. He had a low opinion of the Majorcan doctors: 'The first said I was going to die,' he recalled, 'the second that I had breathed my last, the third that I was already dead.'

In mid-December, evicted from their first lodgings, they moved to an isolated monastery at Valldemosa, to which a Pleyel piano was at length delivered from Paris. There, while George coped with the domestic chores, Chopin worked on his C sharp minor Scherzo, C minor Polonaise and F sharp Impromptu, as well as completing his 24 Preludes. In February 1839 they left for Marseilles then spent the summer at Nohant.

Archiv für Kunst und Geschichte

Chopin (left) painted in 1848 – a year before his death. It was in this year that he performed his last concert in Paris at the Salle Pleyel and saw George Sand for the last time, quite by accident. He was, by this time, seriously ill.

A productive period

Life fell into a pattern: summers they usually spent at Nohant, otherwise they each maintained a Paris apartment. Chopin had given no public concerts since March 1838, when he played his E minor Concerto at Rouen to honour a compatriot, the conductor Orlowski; in the same month he had played before Louis Philippe at the Tuileries. He was to give another command performance for the royal family in October the following year, this time at St Cloud with the Prague-born pianist Moscheles. Moscheles had at first thought Chopin's music 'rather cloying' and 'unmanly', but had since become an ardent admirer. Shortly afterwards Chopin played him his first mature sonata, in B flat minor.

When he was not giving lessons or composing, Chopin spent much of his time with George Sand and her children, frequently entertaining at either his place or hers. Besides the usual Polish émigrés, guests included the novelist Balzac, the composers Meyerbeer and Berlioz and the great Romantic painter Delacroix. Though at the height of his creative powers, in the salons of the nobility Chopin tended to be held in higher regard for his gifts as a pianist, improviser and impersonator – of, for example, familiar figures such as Liszt and Kalkbrenner – than for his composing.

He and George were very close at this time: he was a great comfort to her when her first dramatic venture, *Cosima*, failed, and when she accompanied their friend, the mezzo-soprano Pauline Viardot, on a concert trip he and her children stayed behind to look after each other and mourn George's absence.

Rift with George Sand

His health was ever precarious; though 5 feet 8 inches tall, he weighed only six stone thirteen pounds at this time – little more than the 12-year-old Solange. None

Maurice Sand (below right) as drawn by his mother George Sand (below left) before he had grown into an irresponsible and conceited young man with a fierce jealousy of Chopin. He was largely instrumental in bringing the lovers' relationship to its bitter and premature end.

Carnavalet/Telarci-Giraudon

Carnavalet/Lauros-Giraudon

In 1848, after an exhausting round of concerts and lessons in London, Chopin stayed in Edinburgh (above). Increasingly sick and frequently coughing blood, he gave a concert which created so little enthusiasm that Jane Stirling (above right), his devoted admirer, bought a batch of tickets and gave them away.

the less, he suddenly decided to yield to his friends' urgings and give a public performance. Then began 'the Chopinesque nightmare' of doubts, fears and indecision. He tried to cancel the concert when he learned that their beloved Pauline Viardot could not appear with him, and he forbade the printing of posters and programmes. As Marie d'Agoult had once remarked, 'Chopin keeps changing his mind. The only constant thing about him is his cough.'

With George's support, the concert, held on 26 April 1841, was less of an ordeal than Chopin had feared. It was a dazzling occasion, producing excellent reviews ('Chopin has done for the piano what Schubert has done for the voice') and the fantastic sum of 6000 francs in revenue. Another performance, again at the Salle Pleyel, was given the following February, with Pauline Viardot and Auguste Franchomme. Again the occasion was a triumph, audience and reviewers united in their rapture ('sheer poetry superbly translated into sound'). It was Chopin's last but one performance for six years.

His relationship with George Sand began to break down partly when, as her children became young adults, Chopin became caught in the cross-fire of parent-offspring quarrels, and partly because of an extraordinary novel George wrote which plainly mirrored their own relationship as she saw it. In her story the actress Lucrezia Floriani – a virtuous lady, devoted to her children – is destroyed by the jealousy of Prince Karol, the lover whom she has nursed through near-fatal sickness. The implications of this tactless literary venture were obvious to all: George had had enough of her Polish lover. Yet if anything, it was Maurice, George's son, who could most fairly have been accused of jealousy: now an adolescent, he violently resented Chopin's relationship with his mother and had been trying to break it up.

Eventually, after a bitter row in which Chopin tried to arbitrate between Solange, her new husband Clésinger and George, the nine-year friendship was over. Having sent him, on 28 July 1847, a letter of farewell, George was never to seek a reconciliation.

Failing health

From this moment Chopin's health and spirits were on a downward spiral. To give him something other than his pain and misery to think about his friends again persuaded him to give a public concert. He agreed and on 16 February 1848 at the Salle Pleyel he managed to walk unaided to the piano and play not only many of his own compositions but also, to start the concert, Mozart's Trio K496 in E.

A former pupil, Jane Stirling, had been his mainstay and administrator, during the agonizing pre-concert period. Recognizing his need for someone to depend upon, which for so many years George Sand had been, she willingly offered herself in the hope that he would in due course make her his wife. Like George, she was six years older than Chopin, but there the similarity ended. Chopin was grateful to her for her devoted exertions on his behalf but at no time does she appear to have stirred his emotions.

He had long been planning another trip to England and on 20 April 1848, with no thought of the possible risk to his health, he crossed the Channel. Soon, in London, he embarked upon a punishing schedule of social engagements and even went to the opera. He played before Queen Victoria and Prince Albert at a glittering evening at Stafford House, home of the Duke and Duchess of Sutherland.

Desperately ill, Chopin lacked the strength to resist when Jane Stirling suggested a trip to Edinburgh. They left London on 5 August 1848. Neither the 12-hour train journey nor the raw Scottish air did him any good: 'I can hardly breathe,' he wrote to an old friend. 'I am just about ready to give up the ghost.' Yet he survived to give a concert in Manchester (28 August) and to play in Glasgow (27 September) and Edinburgh (4 October). Otherwise his performances were confined to the genteel drawing-rooms of Scottish ladies – all of whom commented that his music sounded 'like water', Chopin reported, while at the same time describing these ladies' own efforts at the keyboard: 'they all look down at their hands while playing and lay the wrong notes with feeling.' Jane Stirling both ored and irritated him, and at last, with the utmost iplomacy, Chopin was able to convey to her, via a elative, that there could be no marriage. Soon afterards, providence gave him an excuse to return to ondon: a charity concert in aid of Polish exiles, held t the Guildhall on 16 November. Though turning out hat night was nearly the death of him, he was little ppreciated by the audience and virtually ignored by he press. Using the English climate as a pretext for eaving 'beastly London' as soon as possible, he arrived ome in Paris, after a seven-month absence, on 4 November.

A brief remission gave him a few more months' elative happiness surrounded by his friends. Some of he inspiration which had deserted him on his break ith George Sand briefly returned, and he produced wo mazurkas which were published posthumously op. 67 no. 2, op. 68 no. 4). But then came the nevitable relapse. His friends moved him to Chaillot, hen outside Paris, for the summer, from where he rote asking his sister Ludwika to visit him.

She was with him when, at 12 Place Vendôme, he ied on the morning of 17 October 1849.

An elaborate funeral took place at the Madeleine on 0 October, with a full performance of Mozart's equiem – as Chopin had requested.

When he had been buried, three miles away at the ère Lachaise cemetery, Ludwika took his heart back o Poland with her, in accordance with his final wish, nd, carefully wrapped, all the letters he had received om George Sand.

Royal College of Music

A daguerreotype of Chopin in 1849. His artistic life in that year seemed to be as suffocated as his tortured breathing. Barely 39, he wrote two mazurkas but had not the strength to make legible copies of them.

Chopin, in 1849, left his tiny apartment in the Square D'Orléans, first for the cleaner air of Chaillot and then, in August, for a lavish apartment in Place Vendôme (left). To begin with he was well enough to take an interest in the furnishings and décor, but a relapse in September was to prove fatal and on 17 October he died.

LISTENER'S GUIDE

A piano recital

Chopin's solo piano compositions have always been admired for their lyricism, passion and beauty. Formally, they are works of intelligence and balance, while emotionally they are full of feeling and song.

We should be grateful to Chopin's teacher in Warsaw, Józef Elsner. It was Elsner who advised his former pupil, on his arrival in Paris as an ambitious 21-year-old, to concentrate on composing music rather than embarking on a three-year course of study with his idol, the pianist and teacher Friedrich Kalkbrenner:

The ability to play an instrument perfectly – as Paganini does the violin or Kalkbrenner the piano – with all that this ability implies . . . is still only a means to arrive at the expression of thought. The celebrity which Mozart and Beethoven enjoyed as pianists has long since evaporated.

Chopin took his point. From then on, he pursued a career above all as a composer. And before his death at the age of 39, he was to produce a body of work comparable to that of many longer-lived masters. In fact the development of his style was so rapid that with his two piano concertos and his 12 Etudes op. 10, written by the age of 22, we already have acknowledged, mature masterpieces.

Though his output was almost exclusively for piano, Chopin need not be thought of as a limited artist – any more than, say, Wagner or Verdi who both concentrated on opera. For within the range of his solo piano music, this Polish master (who was also, and significantly, half French on his father's side) produced pieces of varying weight and complexity. For example there are the somewhat lighter pieces, which have been called 'salon pieces', after the elegant drawing-rooms in which they were played: in the following pages the G flat major Etude, the three waltzes, the Fantasy-Impromptu and the two nocturnes belong in this category. On the other hand, the G minor Ballade, B minor Scherzo and the 'Heroic' A flat major Polonaise are big concert works of great emotional breadth and subtlety.

Chopin as performer and composer

When he played his own piano music, Chopin allowed himself a good deal of freedom, never (it is said) playing the same piece twice in the same way – for example, varying the speed, volume of tone and even occasionally the notes themselves. His music thus sometimes seems to echo his once-famous keyboard improvisations, in which he actually created music as he

A portrait of Chopin (right) from the original painted by Ary Scheffer in 1847. This was the time of the op. 64 Waltzes (nos. 1 and 2 are on this recital), written when Chopin was seriously ill with tuberculosis.

Ferdinand Keller's painting, entitled Chopin ***(below), reminds us that Chopin's Etudes, besides being works of art, are also piano 'exercises', designed to make the hands more flexible. Each study addresses itself to different problems of technique: the 'Revolutionary' Etude, for example, is mainly a test of left-hand stamina and agility, while the slow Etude no. 3 is for melody-playing.***

went along: in fact he even composed some pieces called 'impromptus'.

Another element of the Chopin style is that of display of 'virtuosity'. This is the use of brilliant passages requiring special technical skill from the pianist – rapid fingerwork, leaps from one point of the keyboard to another, and so on. These give us the same kind of thrill as a gymnastic routine, but can, in the case of lesser composers, sometimes be little more than that. With Chopin, though, a virtuoso passage is always musically justified, fitting the form and content of the piece itself.

Playing techniques in Chopin's time.

The 19th century saw great advances in piano playing technique. Chopin, together with his colleague and contemporary Franz Liszt, was one of the pioneers in this field. In fact an older pianist, Ignaz Moscheles, pronounced the op. 10 Etudes ('studies') to be 'unplayable finger-breaking exercises'. Today, however, they are within the reach (though never the *easy* reach) of skilful professional pianists. Chopin dedicated these op. 10 Etudes to another magnificent pianist, Liszt. But if the Etudes are designed to make strengths of all the player's natural weaknesses, they are above all pieces of music, not just keyboard 'exercises' as many previous studies had been.

Influences

The two main influences on the Chopin Etudes were the violinist Paganini and the pianist Liszt. Paganini's music for unaccompanied violin created new technical standards for the instrument which the young Liszt, in particular, tried to emulate in pianistic terms. Chopin was less dazzled by virtuosity than his Hungarian colleague – their temperaments were very different – but he too was excited by Paganini and above all by Liszt's rapid progress towards becoming a sort of 'Paganini of the piano'. He could at least be sure that Liszt would not find his Etudes 'unplayable' – in fact one of his letters speaks of the marvellous way Liszt played these then very innovative pieces. An eminent critic, on the other hand, advised pianists to have a surgeon standing by before attempting them.

Another important element of the Chopin style is found in the 'dreamier' pieces such as his nocturnes. These exploit something which in pianistic terms is much the same as the *bel canto* ('beautiful singing') style used by operatic singers. Chopin greatly enjoyed good singing, and the kind of full-bodied yet flexible melody that the right hand plays in a nocturne owes much to what he heard in the opera house in Paris. There were piano nocturnes before Chopin (notably by the Irish composer John Field), but Chopin went far beyond his model in depth of feeling and spontaneity. Interestingly, his song-like piano melodies have sometimes attracted words: the op. 10 no. 3 Etude and the Fantasy-Impromptu both lent tunes to 'Tin Pan Alley' a generation ago.

Finally, there is the Polish legacy. In Chopin, this was not simply a vague romantic nostalgia for the homeland which he left as a young man. Throughout his life he composed mazurkas – using a Polish dance form in triple time – and polonaises. In both these forms he quickly learned to convey a wide range of emotions. But though he does very occasionally use a folk melody, for example, in the B minor Scherzo in this recorded recital, he never became a 'nationalist' composer (like some of his contemporaries who felt it their duty to express their country's musical soul). Even at his most Polish – say in the G minor Ballade or A flat major Polonaise – Chopin retains his very individual style.

Chopin's Etudes were influenced and inspired by two of the most flamboyant figures of the contemporary music scene, the violinist Paganini (left) and the pianist/composer Franz Liszt (below). Paganini's 'devilish' mastery of the violin had revealed new potential in the field of musical technique, which Liszt had realized in his formidable piano-playing. Chopin appropriately dedicated his innovative op. 10 Etudes to Liszt.

BBC Hulton Picture Library

Bulloz

Chopin's works, especially his Nocturnes and Etudes, were also greatly influenced by his love of opera, particularly the* bel canto *style of opera of Rossini (above) and Bellini.* Bel canto *– literally 'beautiful singing' – exists in the full-bodied melodies of works like Rossini's* Barber of Seville *(below). Chopin's memorable and often highly 'singable' melodies can be seen as a pianistic equivalent of this operatic style.

Programme notes

In Chopin's time, a whole recital of music given by a single performer was an unusual event, and a whole concert devoted to the works of a single composer equally rare. But since then we have learned that a Chopin recital can provide a superb musical experience, letting us savour his unique gifts of expression across a range of shorter and longer pieces.

Ballade no. 1 in G minor, op. 23

Chopin's First Ballade was sketched in 1831 but not completed until 1835. Like the three other Ballades which were to follow, it may have been inspired by the ballad poems of his compatriot Adam Mickiewicz, although there is no definite literary 'programme' attached to the music. Nevertheless a musical drama clearly unfolds, and one might call this music a 'tone poem' for piano: indeed, such music as this may well have inspired Liszt to compose his 'symphonic poems' for orchestra in later years. Liszt, Grieg and some other composers were also to write piano ballades, but Chopin was the first to use this term (borrowed from an epic, narrative style of poetry) for a piece of music.

The introduction to this first Ballade is slow and ends with the music hanging like a question mark. Then the highly expressive first theme 'creeps in', like a slow waltz, and builds steadily up to a fast, wild passage. This dies away, and there is a sort of 'horn call', alternating two left-hand chords, ushering in the warm (major key) second tune.

Example 1

The rest of the Ballade is built up from these two musical ideas. Essentially they are used in alternation and also through various keys. Much of the sheer dramatic tension arises from this harmonic 'straying' from the home key of G minor, and this tension is hardly released by the especially fast and furious *coda* (closing section) played *Presto con fuoco* (at a faster, fiery tempo) and culminating in rushing scales. On the way, however, the two themes undergo what amount to a series of 'costume changes', appearing sometimes in ballroom splendour (the second theme on its appearance just before the central section), sometimes in dark, mysterious

Reg Wilson

Giraudon

Chopin's Ballades were inspired by the passionate **Lithuanian Ballades** *of Adam Mickiewicz (left), Poland's greatest poet, or, as Liszt described him, 'The Dante of the north'.*

The light-hearted Etude op. 25 no. 9, is one of the many Chopin works to be given a nickname – 'Butterfly' (below). Like most of the other names, however, this is not one of Chopin's own, though it aptly expresses the nature of the work. The hands flit lightly over the keys, while playing an unusually 'happy' melody.

Courtesy of Burlington Gallery Ltd

garb (the final statement of the first theme, with a left-hand 'drum-beat' brooding below the right-hand melody). These 'costume changes' contribute greatly to the colour and depth of this passionately expressive music.

Etude in E major, op. 10 no. 3

This Etude, despite its number in the op. 10 set, was the last but one to be composed and bears the date 25 August, 1832. This was considered by Chopin himself to be one of his finest melodies and he apparently asked that it should be played at his funeral. Technically, it may be thought of as an exercise in *cantabile* (singing style) playing, the pianistic equivalent of the vocal *bel canto* – and the tune must be carefully shaped and sustained above the gently moving accompaniment. Emotionally, it is a love-song, full of yearning, built on two themes. The impassioned central section is highly contrasted and involves awkward stretches for the hands. However, when this much faster music calms down a most beautiful passage ensues, leading into a restatement of the melody first heard at the opening.

Etude in G flat major, op. 25 no. 9

This light-hearted piece, written in 1832–34, is often called the 'Butterfly' Study. The key, G flat major, means that much of the playing is on the black notes of the keyboard. That in itself does not add to the difficulty, though: the challenge of this piece is to maintain an effortless lightness (Chopin marks it *leggiero,* 'light') while negotiating large, tricky leaps with the left hand as well as playing the dancing tune in the right. (The right hand is throughout stretched to its utmost, too.) The music builds at one point to a very loud climax, which is marked 'passionately', but this is very brief and the ending is shimmering, almost feather light.

Nocturne in E flat major, op. 9 no. 2

This gentle piece is one of the most loved of Chopin's 20 or so Nocturnes. He was still only about 20 years old when he composed it and was certainly inspired to do so by the nocturnes of John Field – mood pieces evoking candlelit evenings in elegant drawing-rooms. The characteristic style is of a flowing and ornate right-hand melody accompanied by a rippling or chordal left hand. Chopin's delicately romantic tune is at first quite simply presented, but becomes steadily more ornamented and passionate. Then, at the point where his audience would have expected the piece to draw quietly to its conclusion, there is a surprisingly powerful climax. Chopin eventually provides the quiet ending, but only after a brilliant flourish, high in the right hand, has transfixed the listener, held him almost in a state of suspended animation, for several tense seconds: only then does he bring the piece to its wonderfully calm conclusion.

Scherzo no. 1 in B minor, op. 20

This is another early Chopin work (1831), and the first of the four scherzos he was to write. The style is a far cry, however, from the original meaning of the word, which implied something playful and humorous. 'How is gravity to clothe herself,' asked the composer Schumann of this work, 'if jest goes about in such dark veils?'; and the English edition of the music actually subtitled it *The Infernal Banquet.*

Chopin marks the music to be played *con fuoco* ('with fire') and the mood is wild indeed, the pianist's fingers flying over the keys. But a middle section brings a respite and a totally different mood. Here Chopin seems almost to exorcize the fury of what has gone before with an utterly simple, gentle tune in the major key: in fact it is a Polish Christmas carol called *Lulajże Jezuniu ('Lullaby Jesu').*

Example 2

But the wild opening music returns, unsatisfied as it seems, and the final page is demonic in its energy.

Grande Valse Brillante no. 1 in E flat major, op. 18

This, like the Scherzo no. 1 in B minor, op. 20 was another of Chopin's early works composed in Vienna in 1831. Vienna, of course, is the home of the waltz and at this time was in the grip of a passion for light, frivolous music – music that could be played while people ate in restaurants or drank wine in the open air. In a letter home, the young Chopin expressed some slight disapproval of this musical taste, calling the waltz composer Strauss a mere 'dance band leader'; but he was too spontaneous a musician to resist the dance for long.

In this E flat major Waltz, perhaps more than any he wrote later, Chopin seems to reflect the fashionable Viennese mood: it is sparkling, jewel-like and suitable (said Schumann) to be danced by countesses. Like the Strauss waltzes, it has a main theme, heard right at the start, which gives way to others hardly less tuneful, only to recur brilliantly later on. These themes alternate with each other like dancing partners until the coda is reached. The dazzling final section begins with a crescendo and closes with music that seems to suggest the dancers waltzing off into the distance.

Valse no. 7 in C sharp minor, op. 64 no. 2; Valse no. 6 in D flat major, op. 64 no. 1

These two waltzes were written around 1846–47, quite near the end of Chopin's life and when he was already very ill with tuberculosis. Both are more graceful, and less boisterous, than the preceding one.

Understanding music: the piano in Chopin's time

As Chopin was entrancing the salons of Paris with his remarkable piano playing, the piano was becoming the most popular of all musical instruments. In 1836, the London piano makers, Broadwood, were making 3000 pianos a year and there was no shortage of pupils willing to learn the king of instruments from one of its undisputed masters. But in Chopin's day, the piano, so familiar us now, was a comparatively new instrument.

The pianoforte had been invented over a century earlier by the Italian Bartolomeo Cristofori, in response to the demand for an instrument with more 'feeling' than the harpsichord. In a harpsichord, the strings are plucked, and the way a player hits a note has no effect on its loudness. With the pianoforte, the strings are hammered, and the player can play a note softly *(piano)* or loud *(forte)* to suit the mood of the music.

But like its predecessor, the clavichord, the early piano had a weak tone, and was no match for the harpsichord in the concert hall. It was not until about 1790 that the harpsichord was really overtaken by the piano. By then, composers such as Mozart were writing music specifically for piano and the piano was established as the centrepiece of the composer's armoury. Yet the potential of the piano had barely begun to be tapped.

Over the next 30 years, pushed both by the demands of performers and composers like Beethoven and the technical innovations of the piano makers, the piano (and piano music) developed a power and range of expression almost inconceivable to the keyboard exponents of Mozart's day. Improvements to the piano were made in three main areas.

First of all, the piano became physically much stronger so that it could stand up to the demands of increasingly vigorous performances – Liszt in particular was renowned for breaking pianos during his concert tours in the 1820s. Piano makers began to use metal to strengthen the frame over which the strings were stretched. By the 1850s, cast iron frames were the norm.

The sound of the piano was also changed in a number of ways. In early pianos, the hammer that struck the strings had been covered in hard leather. This gave a clear but rather hard and thin tone. But in 1820, Jean-Henri Pape, who worked for the Paris piano makers Pleyel, patented felt coverings. These, combined with tempered steel strings, gave a much fuller, softer tone.

Finally, the action of the piano was also developed to make it a remarkably versatile instrument. The greatest innovation was the *double escapement* invented b[y] Sebastien Erard. It is the 'escapement' tha[t] pulls the hammer back from the string[s] once they have been struck. In Mozart'[s] day, the hammer had to be pulled righ[t] back from the string before the note coul[d] be played again and rapid repitition of [a] note was impossible. Erard's doubl[e] escapement meant that the hammer ha[d] only to come a little way back before th[e] note could be played again, allowing th[e] pianist to play fast trills as never before.

Equally significant was the dramati[c] increase in the range of the piano. I[n] Mozart's day it was a mere five octaves; i[n] Beethoven's it increased to six; and by th[e] time Chopin reached Paris it was a ful[l] seven octaves, enabling him to contras[t] deep bass sonorities with high trebl[e] filigree passages.

With these changes, the piano becam[e] the complete instrument, equally at hom[e] entertaining in the parlour as dominatin[g] the concert hall, capable of expressin[g] anything from soft lyricism to thunderou[s] anger. Above all, the changes allowed th[e] emergence of the piano virtuoso, a singl[e] performer of genius with the power of the symphony orchestra and the subtlety o[f] expression of the solo violin at his fingertips.

The Valse no. 7, in particular, suggests ballet rather than the ballroom.

Both pieces are in the kind of alternating-section form that Chopin favoured for his waltzes, the C sharp minor being the more elaborate of the two: its shape may be summarized as A, B, C, B, A, B, with A being the main theme, B the rippling sequence of rapid notes in the right hand and C being the slower, sensuous, song-like section in the major key. The 'Minute' Waltz has a simpler A, B, A shape: the lyrical tune of the middle section was once made into a popular song called 'Weep No More'. Incidentally, it was never Chopin's idea that it should be played within a minute, at which speed it becomes too much of a rush.

Etude in C minor, op. 10 no. 2

This is the famous 'Revolutionary' Study. It may have been inspired by the disastrous news of a Warsaw uprising and its suppression by the Russians which occurred in September, 1831. We know that Chopin heard of these events when in Stuttgart and was terribly upset and anxious for his family and friends; what is less proven is the legend that he instantly sat down and wrote this passionate music – in fact, some writers have claimed that the piece was

Chopin gives a piano recital (left) in the ideal setting for his music – the intimate ambience of the salon (drawing-room).

The Broadwood piano presented to Chopin when he visited England in 1848.

written a year earlier.

Whatever its inspiration, though, the mood certainly fits the story. A flurry of notes in the left hand cascades under right-hand chords and (later) under a searing melody. The whole piece gives a tremendous feeling of ebb and flow, occasionally relaxing only to storm and protest yet more vehemently. But for the pianist who plays this music, there is little respite technically and much left-hand stamina is needed.

Fantasy-Impromptu in C sharp minor, op. 66
This piece was composed in 1835, but Chopin left it unpublished, possibly because he felt it was too much like a work (Impromptu in E flat major) by another composer, Moscheles. Today it is one of his most popular pieces. Over a rippling bass, the right hand plays a tune (if it can be called a tune) consisting of rapid notes in a steady pattern; later, certain notes stand out and a more 'hummable' melody emerges. A middle section that seems totally different in mood and theme proves on close listening to be a variant, at a much slower pace, of the initial rapid-note tune, a poignant love-song now in the major instead of the minor key: the mood here is like that of Chopin's nocturnes, dreamily romantic. The rushing music returns once more, but just before the end we hear the romantic middle-section melody in the left hand, singing out like a farewell.

Nocturne no. 5 in F sharp major, op. 15 no. 2
This is another early piece, perhaps written in 1831. Its form is very straightforward (A, B, A). The tune we hear at the beginning is wonderfully relaxed, even languorous; as in the E flat major Nocturne earlier in this recital, it tends to become more and more ornamented as a melody line as the piece progresses. Indeed, in this piece the pianist has a chance to shine with pearly finger technique in some marvellously delicate filigree writing for the right hand. In the middle section the music becomes fast and urgent, building through a long crescendo to an agitated climax. The loudness then subsides for a return of the first tune, and the piece ends with an elegant descent, in steps, towards a rustling final chord.

Polonaise no. 6 in A flat major, op. 53
A polonaise, as the name suggests, is Polish. But it was not so much a dance as a ceremonial, stately walk, sometimes even equestrian. There is always something of 'pomp and circumstance' about a polonaise, and something strongly patriotic too. Some of Chopin's polonaises, particularly those in a minor key, are sombre as well as

Chopin's op. 64 Waltzes, though inspired by the Viennese model, are much less boisterous in character. They have the grace and poise of Renoir's waltzing partners (right).

Pierre Auguste Renoir 'La danse à la ville'. Jeu de Paume/Réunion des Musées Nationaux, Paris/© Spadem 1982

Robert Harding Picture Library

Chopin's life-long love of Polish dance forms and his identification with Polish folk-music (above) were used in his Polonaises, works of sometimes heroic dimensions.

Whistler's Nocturne in Blue and Gold *(left) is an attempt to express visually what Chopin's Nocturnes express in music. Whistler believed the musical term 'to so poetically say all I want to say and no more than I wish'.*

heroic. However, this great A flat major Polonaise is relatively untroubled in mood, although it would not be too fanciful to hear a note of defiance in its powerful gestures and swinging melodies.

An introduction sets a note of expectancy, even urgency; then an irresistible tune is announced over a bounding left-hand accompaniment. There are other subsidiary tunes, but this main melody is what one especially hears and remembers. Now comes a middle section (in E major) in which, over a galloping left hand – for Franz Liszt, 'the thunder of the Polish cavalry' – a right-hand tune is played that suggests the sound of distant trumpet calls.

Example 3

This leads into a somewhat more relaxed, rather wistful passage with a smoothly-flowing right hand. Eventually and quite inevitably, though, the swinging main tune returns triumphantly, in full military splendour, and the ending is one of the most affirmative that Chopin ever composed.

Great interpreters

Tamás Vásáry (pianist)

Ever since he made his first recording of Chopin's music in the early 1960s, Tamás Vásáry has been regarded as one of the finest interpreters of Chopin. His delicate, inductive phrasing, his sensitive touch and his imaginative ear are ideally suited to Chopin's music.

Vásáry was born in Debreczen in Hungary in 1933 and showed his talent at a remarkably early age, but family circumstances prevented him from studying at the Liszt Academy in Budapest until after the war. There, he was befriended by the composer Kodály who bought him a Steinway piano and shared half his pupils with the young pianist.

The political changes in Hungary dealt a severe blow to the family fortunes and Vásáry was forced to support them, working as an accompanist and playing in cabarets and jazz clubs. When his family had to leave Hungary after the 1956 uprising, it seemed he might have to give up his musical career altogether. But American pianist Annie Fischer, whom he had played with while on a Soviet state tour, secured for him a grant from Deutsche Grammophon. His recordings of Liszt's piano music were acclaimed by critics, and widespread recognition quickly followed, with concerts in Berlin, Vienna, London and New York and many television and radio performances. When, in 1965, Vásáry recorded eight discs of Chopin's music, the critics were ecstatic. His reputation as an interpreter of Chopin was firmly established – our recording dates from this period.

Since then, Vásáry has toured the world and played with nearly every major orchestra. He now lives in Switzerland and has been naturalized Swiss since 1971. But wherever he plays, his technical virtuosity, his freshness of approach and his delicate, Romantic style mean that he is always well received.

FURTHER LISTENING

Piano Concerto no. 2 in F minor, op. 21

While producing relatively few orchestral works, Chopin wrote two of the most brilliant and beautiful piano concertos in the Romantic canon. His second Concerto, written in 1829, amply demonstrates the composer's flair for orchestration and for finding a true balance between soloist and ensemble.

Piano Sonata no. 2 in B flat minor, op. 35

Chopin's second Sonata encompasses an astonishing range of emotions and technique. It is written in four movements. The first two demonstrate dazzling feats of pianistic virtuosity and mercurial changes of mood. The third movement, the *March Funèbre,* is perhaps Chopin's most famous piece of music.

Etudes (1–12 op. 10, 13–24 op. 25, 25–27 op. posth.)

The group of piano pieces known as the Etudes – literally, 'studies' – are often seen as containing all of the features which made Chopin a brilliant and unique composer for the piano. Written largely over a period of seven years between 1829 and 1836, they have been a major influence on later generations of composers. Combining as they do breathtaking pianism with passages of extreme sensitivity, each Etude confronts the performer with a particular challenge to his own technique and personal powers of expression.

IN THE BACKGROUND

'July Paris'

For the talented and successful, the Paris that Chopin knew provided unrivalled opportunity and stimulus. For the less fortunate, however, it was still a city of great hardship and poverty.

In 1831 Chopin arrived in Paris, the city where he was to spend most of his remaining years and, at that time, the undisputed centre of political and artistic activity for all Europe. Scene of both the 1789 revolution and the recent 'July Revolution' of 1830, which set up Louis Philippe as 'citizen king', Paris seemed to embody the spirit of political struggle and to represent all that was progressive in art and thought. It was a place that held a magnetic attraction for refugees and exiles of all kinds, but especially for creative artists, and it provided an ideal setting for the formulation of the ideals of the Romantic movement.

The capital represented opportunity and enterprise. Paris had shrugged off its Imperial past and the years 1830–50 witnessed a rapid expansion in industry and trade and a dramatic increase in the power of the middle class – acquisitive, materialistic and socially ambitious.

Gifted personalities

Chopin was not the only aspiring celebrity of the day to be setting his sights on Paris: 1831 was the year that Aurore Dudevant (better known by her pen-name – George Sand) arrived to lead a new life, away from her husband and, she hoped, in a free and stimulating environment that would prove conducive to her forging a career as a writer; Mendelssohn, too, chose this year to return to the city where six years previously Cherubini had given his blessing to the brilliant 16-year-old's ambition to become a professional musician; others, like the young writer Balzac, had been settled in Paris for some years waiting to make the hoped-for breakthrough with 'a pretty woman he has never met, (whose) name is Fame'.

These three were only a few of the personalities with whom Chopin was to meet in Paris. Soon after his arrival in September 1831 he reported to a friend that he had met Rossini, Cherubini, Baillot (a rival of Paganini's), and the pianists Herz, Hiller, Kalkbrenner and Liszt, and he had seen Meyerbeer's first major success, *Robert le diable*: 'a masterpiece of the modern school . . . I doubt whether anything so magnificent . . . has ever before been done in the theatre.'

Meyerbeer had waited some years for his Paris success. What made *Robert le diable* such a triumph was that it provided in abundance the thrills and spectacle sought by the bourgeois audience of the Opéra. Titillation and conspicuous expense, rather than its impressive and often original orchestration, gave the work an irresistible appeal that had somehow eluded Meyerbeer in his previous attempts to please the Parisian public; now he had the right formula his

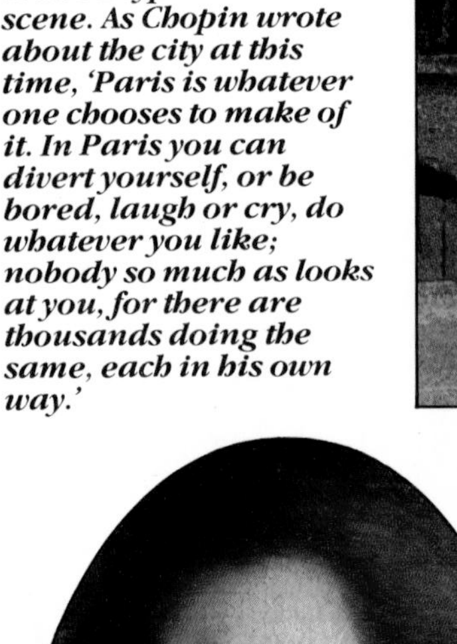

Painted in 1831, the year Chopin arrived in Paris, the watercolour (right) shows a typical Parisian scene. As Chopin wrote about the city at this time, 'Paris is whatever one chooses to make of it. In Paris you can divert yourself, or be bored, laugh or cry, do whatever you like; nobody so much as looks at you, for there are thousands doing the same, each in his own way.'

Mauro Pucciarelli

Louvre/Lauros-Giraudon

Louvre/Bulloz

Thomas Shotter Boys 'La rue vieille du Temple'. Carnavalet/Bulloz

Private Collection/Giraudon

Versailles/Giraudon

Paris in the 1830s and 40s was a centre of artistic creativity. Many of the gifted writers, artists and musicians were also friends and met frequently. Chopin (far left) counted among his contemporaries (from left to right) Delacroix, a major painter of the Romantic movement whose famous self-portrait this is; Lamartine, one of the key literary and political figures of the day; de Musset, celebrated writer and former lover of George Sand, and finally Berlioz, whom Chopin esteemed as a friend but detested as a composer.

Parisians found many ways of entertaining themselves, depending on their social class and interests. The better-off might attend a musical evening in a salon as shown in this unfinished sketch (right). Standing in front of the hearth is the painter Delacroix with the poet de Musset beside him.

new-found fame was secured.

George Sand's experience as a novelist and playwright was in some ways comparable: her first success, *Indiana* (1832), seemed to suggest that women should desert their husbands and children and forget about marriage; the explicitly erotic *Lelia* (1833) furthered her reputation as a daring new talent. These books established Sand as one of France's most popular writers, overshadowed though she was by her contemporaries such as Victor Hugo (*Notre Dame de Paris,* 1831), Balzac (*Eugénie Grandet,* 1833), Stendhal (*Le Rouge et le Noir,* 1830) and the poet Lamartine.

The poet Alfred de Musset, who with Hugo, Lamartine, Vigny and Chateaubriand would be classed among the great literary figures of the Romantic movement in France, was one of George Sand's lovers before she met Chopin: they travelled to Italy together in 1833–34, just as Sand and Chopin were to seek privacy by deserting Paris for Majorca a few years later, and their relationship provided each with raw material for novels.

The literary and artistic circle of Paris was a close-knit one in many ways. They met constantly in each other's homes to discuss the issues of the day – social, political and cultural – and almost always there would be music in some form or other to help pass the evening as pleasantly as possible. Chopin was amazed by the number of pianists ('I do not know if any place has more'), and his reaction was echoed by Mendelssohn, who noted in a letter to a friend that he had 'cast himself headlong into the vortex' of sightseeing and

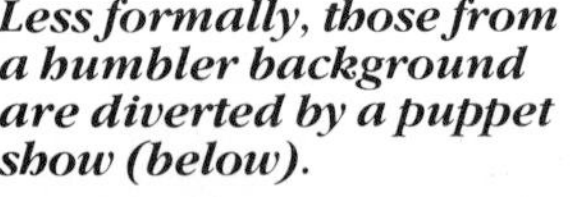

Less formally, those from a humbler background are diverted by a puppet show (below).

ɛ strenuous social whirl: 'Moreover the musicians ·re are as numerous as sands on the sea-shore, all ıting each other; so each has to be visited dividually, and one has to be highly diplomatic ·cause they are all gossips.'

Mendelssohn's favourite theatre was the Théâtre ramatique, which seems to have staged what would ɔw be recognized as variety shows, but he dis-pproved of the fact that politics and sex were so ominent an ingredient of all the acts. He was, ɔwever, enchanted with the Italian dancer Taglioni, hom he saw in *La Sylphide* at the Opéra. The work self perfectly reflected, in its story of a search for an ıattainable ideal, the spirit of the age. Chopin's usic, de Musset's poems, Delacroix's paintings and ugo's novels did the same: the city seemed to breed 'eative artists of the highest calibre, and to provide an nbience in which their work could flourish.

ıe salon

ı the centre of this brilliant section of Parisian society ·as the salon, a name which literally means drawing-ɔom, but which here is used in a wider context to :fer to select social gatherings. It was not enough for ·tists to produce works of art: they had to be seen by ıe opinion-formers of the day, to be part of the ıfluential inner circle.

When Chopin first met George Sand, in 1836, it was ı the presence of Liszt and his mistress Marie 'Agoult, the Polish poet Adam Mickiewicz and the ·riter Sainte-Beuve. And when, about a month later, .hopin invited her to an evening at his apartment in ıe rue de la Chaussée d'Antin, it was in the company f not only Liszt and Marie but of the pianist Pixis, the reat tenor Nourrit, the German poet Heine, and :everal eminent Poles.

Elegant chairs and a Pleyel grand piano furnished :hopin's drawing-room, which had heavy grey urtains and dove-grey wallpaper. On the polished oor, which reflected the light from the candle-lit iano, lay one or two rugs. Liszt played, Nourrit sang nd Chopin improvised on some themes from leyerbeer's latest triumph, *Les Huguenots;* George and, it was noted, said little on this occasion, but sat y the fire and smoked a good deal. After the music, tea vas served and for the rest of the evening Liszt did ıost of the talking.

While such *soirées*, or evening gatherings, were omparatively intimate affairs held in private homes, ıe salon of the musician and piano manufacturer :amille Pleyel was nothing less than a small concert all: a large room with a stage, hung with thick velvet urtains and bedecked with flowers. This was the cene of several of Chopin's Paris concerts given efore the élite of society, who were in Liszt's words he most elegant ladies, the most famous artists, the ichest financiers, the most illustrious lords, . . . a omplete aristocracy of birth, wealth, talent and eauty.'

Chopin, as much as anybody, enjoyed doing the ocial rounds of the aristocracy, visiting the opera and ssociating with talented people. During his courtship f Maria Wodzińska, Chopin had been warned by her arents to avoid, for the sake of his health, late nights n the Paris salons, but he seems not to have heeded he advice.

How could he? He was building his reputation as a nusician and, although since the Revolution the rtistocracy no longer supported their own music taff, reputations still rested largely on the opinion of igh society. In Paris, this meant the residents of the

Carnavalet/Giraudon

The poorer side of Paris is evident in this picture (left) of a coffee seller chatting to her neighbour on the corner of the Porte St Denis.

Bulloz

Masked Parisians (below) enjoy the freedom of Carnival time at midnight.

Markets were a focal point for Parisians. The most famous of all was the vegetable, fruit and meat market of Les Halles shown in this painting (right) of 1835.

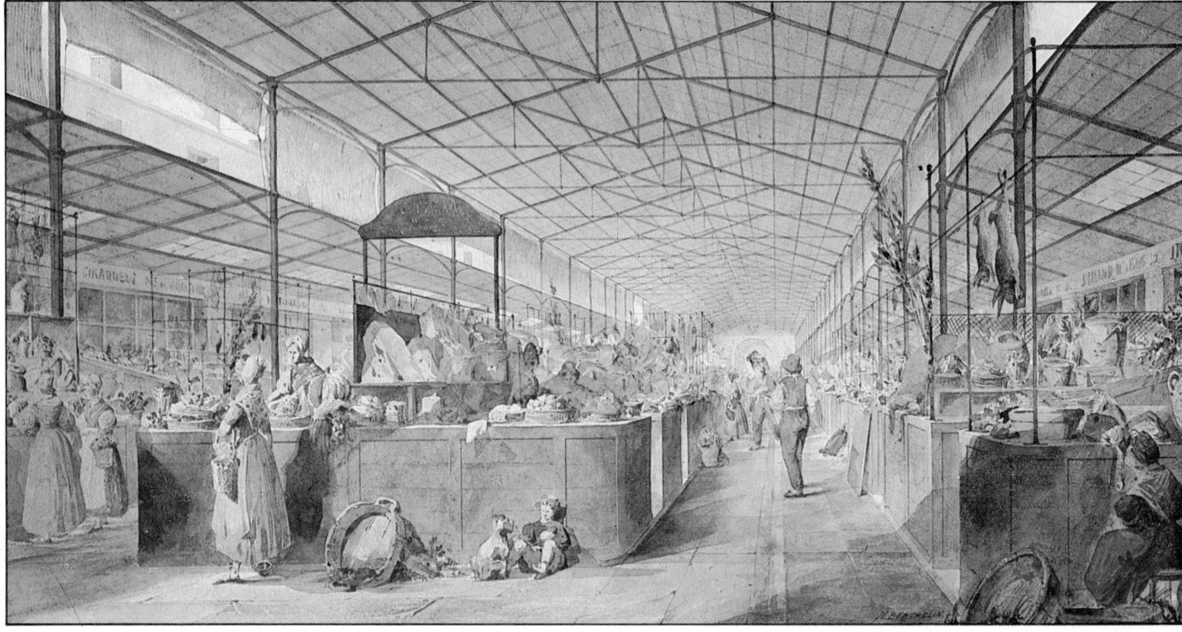

Carnavalet/Salmer

Faubourg St Germain, and everyone knew and accepted this as a fact of life.

As the German poet Heine observed wryly:

The triumphal march of the piano virtuosi is especially characteristic of our time and testifies to the victory of the machine over the spirit . . . Like locusts, the pianists invade Paris every winter, less perhaps to earn money than to make a name for themselves here, from which they can then profit all the more richly in other countries. Paris to them is a huge hoarding on which their fame is spelt out in giant letters . . .

However, Chopin, lacking the constitution of Liszt, could never have lived the life of a touring concert virtuoso. He was also temperamentally unsuited to such a career, preferring to play for small numbers. His very occasional concert performances, despite the high prices charged for tickets, would never have provided him with sufficent income to live in the style necessary for those who wished to be accepted in the salons of the nobility – and it was in these very salons that Chopin made the contacts he needed to attract wealthy pupils. Teaching was his main source of income throughout his adult life, and he depended on being able to command a high fee for lessons.

Among the other expenses Chopin had to meet was that of an apartment well enough furnished and decorated to be suitable for teaching pupils from well-to-do backgrounds, and in an acceptable district. Then there was his carriage, and the hire of a coachman. Perfume was another necessary luxury. There may appear to be an element of dandyism in these extravangances, but this was common to all the members of Chopin's circle.

The other Paris

There was, of course, another Paris – the Paris of the ordinary people, who got up at five every morning and trudged through the mud and filth of the unpaved city streets to dingy workshops and offices in which the smell of the streets permeated the atmosphere and where outbreaks of cholera often spread like wildfire.

Chopin took great delight, as a newcomer to Paris, in walking the streets and observing all aspects of the city that Balzac had summed up as 'mud studded wit[h] diamonds', a vast and exciting place in total contrast t[o] Warsaw. He noticed that once dusk had fallen:

. . . all you hear is street vendors shouting out the titles of the latest pamphlets, and you can often bu[y] three or four sheets of printed rubbish for a sou, such as 'How to Get and Keep a Lover', or 'Priests in Love', or 'Romance of the Archbishop of Paris and the Duchesse de Berry', and a thousand similar

Carnavalet/Salmer

The flower market on the banks of the Seine (right) was a place where the well-to-do mingled with ordinary working people.

scenities very wittily put together.

Crime, of course, increased as darkness gathered. bbery and murder on the streets was a common currence, which the police tended to ignore. To be t of doors on foot after dark was to run a great risk, d most of the young men carried weapons.

Chopin was well aware of the different facets of life Paris:

u find here the greatest splendour, the greatest th, the greatest virtue and the greatest vice; at every p you see posters advertising cures for venereal sease – there is shouting, uproar, noise and mud st anything you can imagine. You can get lost in is swarm – and that's no bad thing: no one quires how anyone else manages to live . . .

The most common form of transport, still, was the rse. Carriages were owned only by the rich. wever, the omnibus had been introduced in areas here the roads were passable. The Champs-Elysées this time was still a country road, with sewage tches at either side. When Chopin first arrived in ris, it was used for grazing cows, and sometimes for ldiers' encampments, though by 1848 about half of had been built on.

The legacy of Napoleon was everywhere – in the 60 w streets, including those near the Louvre and the ileries and in the new bridges over the Seine. On 15 ecember 1840 the cry of *'Vive l'Empereur!'* was ce again heard in Paris, when the French honoured s memory by bringing his remains back from the and of St Helena where he had died nearly 20 years eviously. Nostalgic for past glories, the people were about to re-gild the Napoleonic myth, and it seemed as if most of them had turned out that bitter winter's day to watch the funeral procession pass down the Champs-Elysées.

Bildarchiv Preussischer Kulturbesitz

Street entertainers are still popular with crowds in Paris. The juggler shown above was painted in 1832, the year after Chopin arrived in Paris.

End of an era

Even as this ceremony took place, the nephew of the dead emperor, languishing in prison in northern France after an unsuccessful attempt to overthrow the so-called 'July Monarchy' of Louis Philippe, was

Carnavalet/Lauros-Giraudon

In 1840 the remains of Napoleon were brought back from St Helena and buried with great ceremony at Les Invalides (left). This was in accordance with Napoleon's wishes to be buried on French soil 'in the midst of the French people whom I have loved so well.' In commemoration of the occasion Mozart's Requiem was sung. It was rarely performed in Paris and the next time would be at Chopin's own funeral in 1849.

The army attacks a barricade in the rue St Antoine (below) during the 'June days'. This outburst of popular fury in the summer of 1848 was due to the newly-elected government's decision to abolish the national workshops which administered poor relief. Bands of workers roamed the street singing the* Marseillaise, *barricades sprang up and pitched battles took place. Many workers were massacred or executed after the event. The violence shown by both sides ended all hopes of a stable and democratic republic in France at that time. Chopin's Paris was no more.

plotting his campaign to seize the office that he regarded as his by right. Louis Napoleon Bonaparte's day was not so far away.

There had always been an undercurrent of political unrest in Paris, and political discussion was by no means confined to intellectual circles. The Paris police were more concerned with political offences than with street crime, so that those who read the newspapers in the cafés made sure that they read all of them, in order that their political persuasions should not be generally known.

Gradually the general unrest became, throughout France, stronger and more focused. The frenzy to construct new railways had overreached itself, leaving 50,000 railway workers unemployed in France alone, and this – together with the negative effects of the Industrial Revolution (which was slow to affect France), the economic depression and the failure of the harvest – had made unemployment a major issue.

In early 1848 riots broke out. The National Guard was used to suppress them, but on 22 February, a week after Chopin's last Paris recital at the Salle Pleyel, the Tuileries were stormed. Louis Philippe had already fled. The direct outcome of the uprising was the installation in December that year of Louis Napoleon as President. He would later be known as Napoleon III, after a democracy lasting less than four years, and France under the Second Empire would be run according to principles which had much in common with those of both the first Napoleon's dictatorsh and the autocratic rule of Louis Philippe.

For Chopin and his colleagues, the immedia outcome of the 1848 Revolution was that he no long had any means of making a living. As Berlioz observ in his *Memoirs:*

Who thinks of art at such a time of frenzy and carnage? Theatres shut, artists ruined, teachers unemployed, pupils fled; pianists performing sonatas at street corners . . . painters sweeping gutters, architects mixing mortar on public buildin sites . . .

It was the end of an era. Liszt gave up his conce career and became director of music to the Duke Weimar. George Sand remained at Nohant. The aili Balzac returned briefly to Paris the following year die. Victor Hugo, who at first held office in the ne régime, fled to Brussels in 1851, the year of the cou d'état.

Chopin's Paris was no more, though he did not li long enough to suffer directly from the soci consequences of the uprising: his suffering, England, Scotland and finally in Chaillot and Paris, w to take another form. Perhaps it was as well. The ne order – to be known as the age of the bourgeoisie a epitomized in the novels of Zola as Philistine, selfi and money-grubbing – was not one in which a tale such as his could easily have flourished.

Lauros-Giraudon

THE GREAT COMPOSERS

Franz Liszt

1811-1886

Liszt was not only the greatest piano virtuoso of his age but also a composer of immense originality who had a powerful influence on the Romantic movement. From his first tour, begun when he was only 12, to his last, when he contracted fatal pneumonia, his dazzling techniques overwhelmed his audiences – especially women, for whose company he felt a recurrent need. Influenced by Paganini's violin virtuosity, Liszt in turn encouraged younger Romantics, above all Wagner, whom he helped financially and with his pen. Although Wagner's adultery with Liszt's daughter, Cosima, estranged the two men for a time, they were reconciled in 1870 when Wagner married Cosima, and Liszt regularly attended the Bayreuth festival. As a composer, Liszt wrote little before the 1830s, but from then on he produced a stream of works, especially for the piano. His later works were mainly sacred music – appropriately, as he became an **abbé** ***in 1865. His very last pieces anticipate the atonality of Schoenberg or Webern.***

Both in his lifetime and, to a lesser degree, since his death, Liszt's truly staggering virtuosity as a pianist, and the highly theatrical nature of his performances, have tended to distract attention from his own works. But as the following pages make clear, Liszt decided in 1848 to give up his role as a virtuoso – temporarily, as it transpired – and concentrate on composing. From this period at Weimar date his symphonic poems, the Hungarian Rhapsodies, a mass of solo piano music and the two Piano concertos – all analyzed in the Listener's Guide *– which have remained popular parts of the repertoire. The middle decades of the 19th century saw the transformation of the travelling musician from a superior servant into a virtuoso – an almost godlike figure at whose demonic performances men, and especially women, swooned in rapture. In this, Liszt, as* In the Background *makes clear, was emulating Paganini, the very first of the musical 'superstars'.*

COMPOSER'S LIFE

'A god amongst us'

Virtuoso extraordinary, passionate lover, man of religion and composer of genius, Liszt's sensational career embodied the ambitions, contradictions and achievements of the Romantic movement

Carl Czerny (right) was Beethoven's most brilliant pupil and, in turn, one of the young Liszt's most important teachers in Vienna. He was also a composer of repute, though today he is best remembered as a composer of several instructive works for the piano.

Liszt (below) at the age of 16. By this early stage in his long and eventful career, Liszt was already an acclaimed and experienced piano virtuoso.

Royal College of Music

Franz Liszt, or Ferencz, as he was christened, was born in the small village of Raiding in Hungary on 22 October, 1811. It was the year of the Great Comet and the gypsies who camped nearby foretold a dazzling future for the baby. His father, Adam Liszt, was a land steward on the estates of Prince Esterházy: Haydn had served at the Esterházy court for 30 years: Mozart's pupil Hummel had been Kapellmeister there; and Cherubini had been a visitor. Adam himself could play most instruments and bought his son a piano as soon as he was big enough to sit on a piano stool.

Under his father's tuition the boy made outstanding progress. At the age of nine he made his first appearance in public, stealing the thunder from a titled blind pianist who was top of the bill. Shortly afterwards he caused a sensation with a solo performance at the Esterházy home. The Princess was so impressed that she gave him Haydn's name book – unfortunately for posterity, the child promptly lost it. His first newspaper review declared his playing 'beyond admiration'. A group of local dignitaries formed a committee and provided the young genius with a six-year stipend so that he could study.

Adam was so ambitious for his son that he resigned his post and, with his wife Anna, left Hungary for Vienna, the musical capital of Europe. Here he tried to engage the services of Hummel as a teacher, but found him too expensive. Instead, he settled for Salieri, the man who had been responsible for so much of Mozart's misfortune, and the composer Czerny, who was Beethoven's greatest pupil. Czerny was so amazed at the potential of the young Liszt that he refused to accept any fee. He noticed with astonishment that 'Nature had produced a pianist.' Liszt could play anything at sight and improvised brilliantly though he knew nothing of harmony. He was such a sickly child (this was attributed in part to the fact that his mother had fallen down a well shaft when she was pregnant) that his exertions nearly made him fall off the piano stool; and he had the most alarming habit of 'flinging his fingers all over the keys'. Czerny set out to give the boy what he lacked – control and discipline – but the

Archiv für Kunst und Geschichte

'flying fingers' remained a hallmark of his playing, ar an innovation, because until Liszt pianists had play in the same way as organists, with their fingers curl under like claws.

'It is Mozart himself'

At this time Liszt was presented to Beethoven. intermediary persuaded the musical giant of the day attend one of Liszt's concerts, and though there some doubt as to whether Beethoven would ha accepted, being very deaf, Liszt himself often told t story of how, when he had finished playing, Beethov got up on to the stage and embraced and kissed hi Ungenerous critics have dismissed this symbo encounter as pure invention. But Liszt needed no su publicity: his Viennese concerts brought a rash of ra reviews. 'A young virtuoso has dropped from the clouds,' they gushed, 'There is a god amongst us.'

When Liszt was 12, Czerny declared there was no more he could teach him and recommended that he should continue his studies at the Paris Conservatoire. Before travelling to Paris Liszt gave a farewell concert in Budapest and repaid the sum he had been donated. Then there was a triumphant tour of Germany: in Munich he received a second portentous kiss, this time from the monarch.

Initially, Paris was disappointing. Cherubini, director of the Conservatoire, upheld the rule that foreigners were not to be admitted. But there was a compensation: Sébastian Erard, the famous piano manufacturer, had heard of the young Liszt's prodigious success and with an astute sense of the value of publicity he gave him an instrument of the very latest design which permitted rapid repetition of one note. Thus equipped, Liszt took Paris by storm. 'Since last night I believe in reincarnation . . . It is Mozart himself. His tiny arms can scarcely reach both ends of the keyboard, his feet can hardly touch the pedals . . . yet he is the first pianist in Europe,' enthused the press. He played to the French royal family, he was lionized by the noblest ladies of the land and his picture was on sale in every shop. Such was the tumult around him that his mother, a simple countrywoman, decided to return to Austria to live with her sister.

In 1824 Liszt made his London début. The pianist Moscheles, who had every reason to be jealous, generously affirmed that 'in strength and in his conquest of difficulties he surpasses anything hitherto heard.' Exhausting tours of France and Ireland followed, culminating in a royal command performance before George IV at Windsor.

By the time he was 16, Liszt had been in the limelight for seven years and the strain was beginning to tell. He and Adam took a sea cure at Boulogne. Liszt turned for strength to religion, as he was always to do, but his father, also weakened by their travels, fell ill with typhoid and died. His last words to his son were 'Je crains pour toi les femmes' (literally, 'I'm afraid for you and women'). Adam Liszt had a presentiment that women would be his son's undoing or rather that his passion for women would be greater than his dedication to music.

First loves

After the death of his father Liszt was disillusioned by stardom. Believing that his art was 'debased to not much more than a trade . . . labelled as entertainment for fashionable society', he gave up performing and

Julius Muhr 'Gipsy Family'. Schackgalerie, Munich/Joachim Blauel/Artothek

Mauro Pucciarelli

A Romantic vision of a gypsy family (above). Similar images inspired Liszt's* Rhapsodies, *for though the composer – dressed in Hungarian style on the right – left his homeland when he was a boy he never forgot his 'roots'.

George Sand and her coterie (below). Among the men depicted around this highly individual and brilliant woman are the painter Delacroix, who stands behind Sand and the unmistakable Liszt, and the bearded dramatist Félicien Malefille, who is declaiming on the right. Chopin, George Sand's current lover, is represented by the brightly coloured bird perched upon her knee.

Musée Carnavalet/Lauros-Giraudon

Courtesy of the Map House, London

went to live quietly with his mother, who had returned to Paris. His teaching brought in enough money to keep them both.

It was at this time that he first fell in love. Caroline de Saint-Cricq was his pupil, a girl of his own age from an aristocratic family. When the music lessons spilled over into poetry readings her father forbade him to see her again: she was duly married to a diplomat. To Liszt the loss was a severe blow – he suffered an emotional and religious crisis that was to last for two years. (This Caroline was to be the only former love he remembered in his will.) He refused food and felt a strong conviction that his vocation lay with God rather than in music. He suffered cataleptic fits and once, when he was unconscious for two days, a Paris newspaper announced his death and printed an obituary.

In 1830 revolution broke out in Paris. 'The guns have cured him' announced Liszt's mother as her son was aroused from his lethargy. Within the next exciting year he met the three men who were to have a lasting influence on his music: Paganini, Berlioz and Chopin. Paganini's supposed alliance with the devil fascinated the young pianist, as did his uncanny virtuosity. In Berlioz he found another tormented Romantic who had extended the range of the orchestra just as Paganini had extended the range of the violin. Liszt determined to do as much for the piano.

Chopin's influence was different: he calmed Liszt's nerves and introduced him to his first great affair. At an impromptu party at Chopin's home Liszt played into the small hours to a select company of artists: Heine, Delacroix, Rossini, Meyerbeer and George Sand. A sixth guest, Marie d'Agoult, was deeply affected. 'His flashing eyes, his gestures, his smile, now profound and of an infinite sweetness, now caustic, seemed intended to provoke me to an intimate assent.'

The reign of Marie

The Countess Marie was a 28-year-old mother of three children. She was estranged from her husband, a man of limited outlook some 20 years older than herself, and she led an independent life devoted to the serious pursuit of literature and philosophy. Her liaison with Liszt, whose mercurial nature inclined him towards passing affairs and involvement in long-term relationships only with women made of sterner stuff than himself, lasted for 10 years.

To begin with the affair was difficult and scandalous and caused both of them a great deal of anguish. But in 1835 they broke for ever with convention and settled in Switzerland, where their life together became more ordered. There, their first baby, Blandine, was born. Under Marie's influence Liszt studied Goethe and Dante and applied himself to composition. These were the years of the *Années de pèlerinage,* lyrical evocations of his travels with Marie. While he gave free lessons to the young ladies at the Geneva Conservatory, paying as much attention to their charms as to their musical talents, Marie taught him the airs and graces of the fashionable world. In due course, he grew restless to be back among it.

In 1837 in Italy, a second daughter, Cosima, was born. (She was destined to marry first her father's favourite pupil, Hans von Bülow, then the composer he supported and admired so much, Richard Wagner.) Shortly after Cosima's birth Liszt found the excuse he needed to escape from the domestic setting that was becoming increasingly claustrophobic to him. He heard news of floods in the Danube and rediscovered the meaning of the word 'homeland'. 'O my wild and distant country! O my unknown friends! Your cry of pain has brought me back to you.'

Courtesy of the Royal College of Music/David Parker

The Countess Marie d'Agoult (left). Until her relationship with Liszt, by whom she had three children, 'her reputation hadn't a blemish.'

On the road again

He rushed to Vienna and gave 10 concerts to relieve the homeless. He also visited Hungary for the first time since his boyhood and heard once more the music of the gypsies, which had fascinated him since his youth. After a long absence from the stage the adulation he received went straight to his head. Not surprisingly, this was the beginning of the final rift between Liszt and Marie. Although he returned to her, the taste of fame was too sweet and after the birth of their third child, Daniel, he set off on a glittering series of tours that took him all across Europe.

He raised money for a monument to Beethoven, he raised money for charity, and he earned a personal fortune. Everywhere he received the highest accolades: he was welcomed with frenzied enthusiasm; his concerts were a sensation; his presence required speeches and banquets; he was presented with swords, medals, a title; and his departure was attended with solemn ceremony. His coach was often escorted miles out of town by bands of students. If he had to wait five minutes for a train, the station piano would be dragged out onto the platform so that he could perform to the crowd that always surrounded him.

His social success was equally brilliant, for Liszt's prodigious musicianship was matched by his sex appeal. When his face assumed its remarkable agony of expression, mingled with radiant smiles of joy, and his playing reached an impassioned high, ladies would scream and faint, or rush the stage to be nearer his soulful gaze 'like poor little larks, at the feet of a terrible enchanter'. At one concert two Hungarian countesses fell upon each other and rolled over and over on the floor to gain possession of Liszt's snuffbox. At another, a lady retrieved the stub of his cigar – she kept it in her bosom for the rest of her life.

The Swiss scenes and sounds encountered by Liszt on his 'honeymoon' with Marie in 1835 inspired his* Années de pèlerinage, *a sort of musical diary.

As the superstar of the day, he was the darling of courts and salons and wrote to Marie of his conquests. There was Bettina von Arnim, close friend of Goethe and Beethoven: 'an imp of magnetic intelligence'; Charlotte von Hagn: 'the odalisque of two kings'; Princess Belgiojoso; the singer Caroline Unger; the pianist Camille Pleyel; and Mariette Duplessis, la Dame aux Camélias. Sometimes his affairs got out of hand. His liaison with the tempestuous dancer Lola Montez (later the mistress of King Ludwig I of Bavaria) ended when he locked her in their hotel room and beat a hasty retreat out of town.

The mass hysteria that surrounded him – 'Lisztomania' as it was termed – may have done little for Liszt's character as Marie's faithful partner, but it did, once and for all, change the status of the musician in society. Previously, a pianist had been little more than a servant; his playing, background music that filled awkward gaps in the conversation of the audience. Now he was a person to be courted, whose talent entitled him to celebrity status.

But by 1847 the long-suffering Marie had had enough. She ended their relationship in a letter. 'What have I to do with a charming good-for-nothing, an upstart Don Juan, half mountebank, half juggler, who makes ideas and sentiments disappear up his sleeve and looks complacently at the bewildered public that applauds him? Ten years of illusion! Is that not the very sublime of extravagance? Adieu, my heart is bursting with bitterness!' Under the pseudonym of Daniel Stern she wrote a novel, *Nelida* (an anagram of their son's

Musée de l'Opéra/Bulloz

Liszt performs the Galop Chromatique, *the virtuosic stunt with which he nearly always ended his concerts. Addicted to the limelight he returned to the hectic life of a travelling virtuoso in 1839.*

name), in which she portrayed him in a clear and unflattering light. Liszt denounced the book as an unjust attack by a scorned woman, but Marie's fictional account of her lover's weaknesses is more accurate than the fondness his contemporary admirers would allow.

The reign of Princess Carolyne

With Marie eclipsed by other loves, there was now room in Liszt's life for another authoritative woman and in 1847, at the age of 36, he met her. She was Carolyne Sayn-Wittgenstein, a 28-year-old Polish princess who, like Marie before her, was married but separated from her husband. Though Liszt admired her for her title and her wealth, they shared deep religious feelings (Carolyne was also a pious Catholic), a love of literature and a passion for cigars. For the princess it was love at first sight, 'I kiss your hands and kneel before you, prostrating my forehead to your feet, laying, like the Orientals, my finger on my brow, my lips and my heart . . .' She declared that henceforth her whole being existed only to glorify him, and she was as good as her word.

Mauro Pucciarelli

In 1839 Liszt visited Hungary for the first time since his boyhood. He played at Budapest and Poszany, and proposed the foundation of a Hungarian national conservatory. On this, and on his further visits in the 1840s, he was greatly acclaimed. The programme (above) was for a concert given in 1846.

Archiv für Kunst und Geschichte

here was hardly a ountry in Europe to hich Liszt's tours did ot extend. 1847 found im in Constantinople below), where he dmired the views up the osporus and impressed he Sultan.

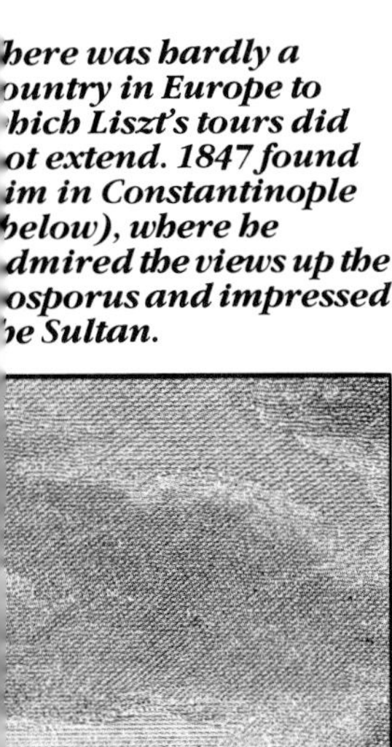

She whisked him off to her romantic castle at Woronince in southern Russia. There, while the snow whirled outside, her servants serenaded the lovers to the playing of the balalaika. In this congenial setting Liszt made a major decision. He renounced his life as a travelling virtuoso and, under Carolyne's encouragement, resolved to devote himself to composition. With this end in mind he went in 1848 to Weimar, where he had had a musical appointment since 1843, to live there permanently on a modest salary as musical director.

There Liszt was joined by Carolyne, who eventually reached Weimar after a dramatic chase to the Russian border, which she crossed only moments before officials closed it at the command of the tsar. (It was difficult for Russian subjects, even aristocrats, and especially independent-minded women, to leave Russia without government permission.) On her arrival, Liszt was obliged to take his leave of the woman who was sharing his hotel room. He joined Carolyne and her daughter, to whom he was more fatherly and affectionate than he was with his own children, in the large villa on the edge of town that was to be their home for the next 12 years. Some visitors did not take kindly to the 'irregular' ménage, but, as usual, the criticism was mainly directed at Carolyne. 'She has ensnared him by his vanity, she strews incense about him perpetually, without proportion and without scruple,' observed one, and Liszt's royal employers continued to address all official correspondence to the hotel where he had initially stayed.

Schloss Nymphenburg, Munich/Joachim Blauel/Artothek

Lola Montez (above) was one of Liszt's most exotic admirers. She once stormed into a banquet where he was present and danced on the table.

But the tough and cultivated princess was more than financially supportive of her genius. Under Carolyne's influence Liszt composed the majority of his best piano works, including the piano concertos. She understood him very well. 'It is not genius that he lacks, but the capacity to sit still — industry, prolonged application. Unless someone helps him in this respect he is impotent, and when the consciousness of his impotence takes possession of him he has to resort to stimulants.' This was the period of his musical maturity and, most important, he used his status there as Europe's foremost musical celebrity to promote the work of other composers, especially that of Richard Wagner. In addition, anybody could attend the free classes he gave three times a week, and everybody did as hordes of aspiring pianists and musicians flocked to Weimar for an 'apprenticeship' under him.

When the divorce proceedings initiated by the princess finally came to a head in 1860, Carolyne went to Rome to get the sanction of the Vatican for their marriage, which was to take place there on Liszt's 50th birthday. But on the eve of the wedding, when the church was already bedecked with flowers, a hooded messenger arrived while Liszt and Carolyne were at prayer and, in true operatic style, announced that the princess's in-laws (her husband was quite equable about the divorce provided his cash settlement was sufficient) had put forward a further objection to the union. The ceremony was duly cancelled. This was a stroke of luck for Liszt, because as his daughter Cosima suggested, it would have been like 'a burial service' to a man who sensed that he had another vocation.

This episode marked a turning point in both their lives. The faith that had united them, now parted them. They were no longer lovers, though they remained close friends. Carolyne took a separate apartment in Rome and, with a supply of cigars at her side, began writing religious works, including an interminable project expressing her disillusionment with the church. It was called *The Interior Causes of the External Weaknesses of the Church in 1870* and ran to 24 volumes. This daunting work took her 25 years to complete, during which time she lived the life of a hermit. Two weeks after she wrote the last word, in 1887, she died.

Retreat to religion

In 1862, the year after the marriage débacle, Liszt's daughter Blandine died in childbirth, and this and the loss of Carolyne turned his thoughts again to religion. Liszt had undergone phases of religious intensity, as a child and – at intervals and with interludes – throughout his life, so the reinvigoration of his faith at this stage in his hectic life came as no surprise to those who knew him well. In 1865 he solemnized this life-long commitment by taking four minor orders of the Catholic church. (A further three vows were required before full ordination as a priest 'licensed' to hear confession and say mass.) He soon moved into an apartment in the fabulous Villa d'Este just outside Rome, where the beauty of the gardens and the famous fountains gave him a perfect environment for composition.

Liszt's new, black-clad and tonsured image as a devout abbé added to his mystique as well as his personal happiness but he was to be disappointed by the reception given to his sacred music: Catholics found it too innovative and in Protestant countries it was regarded with suspicion. Of his new life, he wrote to a confidante, 'I have not changed, it is only that my life is ordered more simply'. That he was the same man was to be proved by the fact that the serene Villa d'Este was the setting for his last dramatic affair.

A young Russian, the 'Cossack Countess', Olga Janina, came to Rome to seduce him. At 19, she already had a colourful past behind her. Her childhood had been devoted to bloodsports and she had lived among thoroughbred horses. She was married at 15. On the morning after her wedding she horsewhipped her

Bethnal Green Museum/Robert Harding Picture Library

Carolyne and her daughter (right). Liszt's relationship with her ended in Rome (above), where he acted on his vocation to be an abbé. But his faith was as aesthetic as it was spiritual.

Roger-Viollet

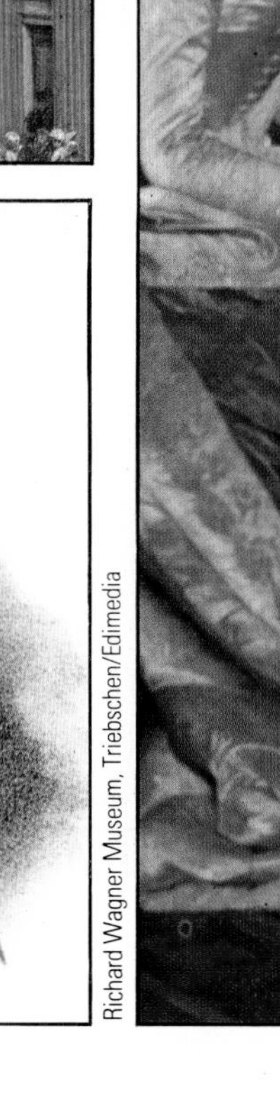

Richard Wagner Museum, Triebschen/Edimedia

Archiv für Kunst und Geschichte

husband and left him. At 16 she bore a daughter. Then she went to study the piano and became infatuated with Liszt's music, and, inevitably the man himself.

Knowing Liszt's weakness for luxury she rented a fantastic apartment and bought a complete wardrobe from the Parisian couturier Worth. Liszt the former womanizer was impressed, but he said, 'Never speak to me of love: I must not love.' Cleverly, she allowed him to retire to the Villa d'Este and gave him enough time to grow lonely in his meditations. Then she appeared at his door dressed as a gardener's boy and bearing a basket of flowers. 'He showed such joy that I could see how terribly solitude weighed upon his soul that was so passionately in love with the world and its homage.' Their relationship was tempestuous. Liszt repented of his lapse from celibacy and refused to see her; Olga threatened to kill them both, to take poison, to slash her wrists; after a week he was again her lover.

The end came when Olga, a would-be concert pianist, bungled three attempts at a recital. Liszt was so harsh with her that the audience was saddened and embarrassed; the poor girl returned home to take a dose of laudanum (tincture of opium) and remained unconscious for 48 hours. She threatened to shoot them both, but he persuaded her to leave. Olga, like Countess Marie, consoled herself by writing a book about Liszt, revealing the division in his personality.

A 'three-cornered existence'

Towards the end of his life Liszt began a strenuous regime, a 'three-cornered existence', dividing his year between Rome, Weimar and Budapest and devoting his time to music, religion and love, not necessarily in that order. The arrangement was satisfactory, but exhausting. Cosima had married von Bülow in 1857 but in 1864 she married Wagner, after a protracted liaison in the course of which she had two children by him. When the scandal first broke Liszt was loyal enough to his first son-in-law to sever relations with Cosima and Wagner for five years. Eventually, however, he was reconciled with them and Wagner's death in 1883 came as a great blow.

It was en route for Bayreuth in 1886 that he caught his death of cold. He was sitting in a train with a honeymoon couple who were admiring the moon through the open window – not a situation a great Romantic would complain about. Once in Bayreuth he fell ill with pneumonia, and died painlessly on 31 July.

Koronázási Mise

LISZT FERENCZ.

Előadva Budan 1867 Szentivan ho 8ᵃⁿ

midőn Ő felségeik

Első Ferencz József

Osztrák Császár

Magyar Ország apostoli királyává

Erzsébet Császárné pedig

Magyar királynévá

koronaztatnak.

SCHUBERTH J. & TÁRSA

Mauro Pucciarelli

As the grave Abbé Liszt, the composer's image in old age was that of the artist as a benign patriarch. Here he is shown in his study (below) where he devoted much of his last few years to composing sacred music (above) and at Bayreuth (left) with Cosima and Richard Wagner. He died there in 1886.

LISTENER'S GUIDE

Piano Concertos

Liszt's dazzling mastery of the keyboard and his love of orchestral effects inspired two of his most important works, the heroic First Piano Concerto and the poetic Second Piano Concerto.

As a pianist, Franz Liszt was a phenomenon. Nobody before or since has ever combined such dazzling technique, such overwhelming charisma and such remarkable musical insight in such generous measures. When Liszt glided to the piano, tossed his hair and brought his hands down in a glittering avalanche upon the keyboard, ladies swooned and shrieked, men wept and other musicians were reduced to gawping.

But Liszt was more than just a mere showman. His mastery of the keyboard was complete. Nothing seemed beyond him. Nobody quite believed that a man with such remarkable powers could ever be a genuine musician as well, and there has been a tendency to write Liszt's piano works off as mere pyrotechnics. The two Piano Concertos in particular have come in for considerable abuse. But both the concertos included some remarkable innovations; they are as complex structurally as any Romantic concerto; and they contain many passages of great beauty and power.

Mauro Pucciarelli

The Piano Concertos

Perhaps the most surprising thing about the Concertos is just how long they took to complete and how many versions they went through. If Liszt ever intended them as showcases for his talent on the keyboard, he changed his mind and tried to make them much more than this, long before they reached the final version.

Liszt did not complete the Concertos until 1849, two years after he had stopped touring as a pianist. Even then, the E flat Concerto was not premièred for another six years, and the A major for another eight. And both Concertos were revised extensively at least twice in the late 1850s.

Liszt first started thinking of writing a concerto when he was barely 19 – it was a natural thing for a piano virtuoso to do. The idea for the opening theme of the First Piano Concerto can be traced to a sketchbook dating from as early, perhaps, as 1831. It may not be a coincidence that Liszt had heard, and been overawed by, the première of Berlioz's *Symphonie Fantastique* only a few months previously. Liszt's theme certainly has an element of the grim devilry that attracted him in Berlioz's music. Ideas for the Second Piano Concerto probably date from the same period.

Immediately afterwards, however, in March 1831, Liszt encountered the Paganini phenomenon and the ideas were abandoned. When he finally returned to them in the late 1830s, he wrote a number of prototypes for both Concertos – indeed the First Piano Concerto may well have been completed in one form. But these early versions are perhaps what could be expected of the 'Paganini of the keyboard'. They are virtuoso display pieces with an incredibly difficult piano part. And, impressive pieces of keyboard pyrotechnics as they are, they have little else to recommend them.

During the 1840s, however, Liszt began to mature musically, and to realize that there was no need for him to stretch the keyboard to its very limits to write an effective piece. Once he took up conducting in Weimar in 1843, he began to develop a keen ear for other instruments in the orchestra and appreciate the importance of proper orchestration.

Liszt and the orchestra

What Liszt tried to achieve in his use of the orchestra in the concerto was, in Schumann's words, 'a new and brilliant [way] to bind the orchestra and piano

Liszt first toyed with the idea of writing a piano concerto when he was just 19, but he did not actually complete his Piano Concertos until he was at the peak of his powers (above). Both works are on a grand scale (right) with their brilliant piano fireworks and massive orchestration.

John Martin 'Design for the Seventh Plague of Egypt'. Laing Art Gallery/Tyne & Wear County Council Museums

Royal College of Music

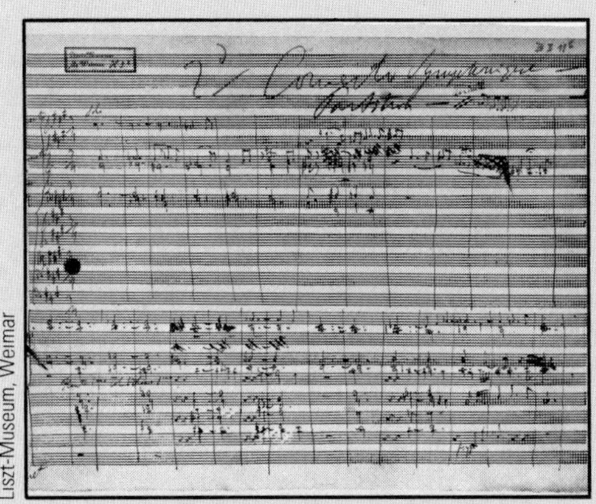

Liszt-Museum, Weimar

Joachim Raff (left), Liszt's secretary from 1849–54, made the extravagant claim that much of Liszt's orchestration was in fact his own. We know, however, that Liszt orchestrated the final versions of both the Piano Concertos: above is the orchestral score of the Second Piano Concerto, in Liszt's own hand.

together.' In the piano concertos of the period, the orchestra had tended to become a mere spectator, watching the piano dazzle the audience and simply filling in the gaps. Liszt sought to redress the balance and make his concerto more 'symphonic' – it is significant that Liszt dedicated the First Concerto to Henri Litolff, a composer who called his own concertos *Concertos Symphoniques.*

In Litolff's concertos, the orchestra carried as many of the musical ideas as the piano itself. Liszt's Concerto takes this approach further, not only matching the massive power of his piano displays with equally massive orchestration exploiting the stridency of brass and all the rhythmic effects at his disposal, but also by giving orchestral instruments solo passages to match the delicacy of the piano's more lyrical moments.

Of course, Liszt could never neglect the display element. Indeed, he believed it was essential to a concerto. When Schumann initially called his Sonata in F minor a *Concerto without Orchestra,* Liszt insisted that a concerto was 'a piece for public performance' and so needed 'brilliant expression and grand style'. And true to form, Liszt wrote plenty of piano fireworks into his Concertos.

One movement

The most significant innovation in the Concertos, however, is the fact that there are no real movements as such. Although the First Concerto can be broken into four main sections, they run into each other without a break; there are no real divisions in the Second Concerto at all.

In writing a successful single movement concerto, Liszt provided a solution to the problem that had plagued the Romantics ever since they had rebelled against the rigidity of Classical forms and their strict movements. Without the rigid form, it was difficult to maintain a sense of unity over a long piece of many contrasting moods.

Liszt's solution was 'thematic transformation' – that is, one theme would appear again and again during the course of the concerto, transformed each time but sufficiently recognizable to hold the piece together. The idea was not entirely new. Schubert had used it in his *Wanderer Fantasy.* Berlioz's use of repeated motifs (the *idée fixe*) where a particular tune on a particular instrument represents a character, hints at it. And other composers had dabbled with the idea. But Liszt was the first to use it so thoroughly and so successfully.

Programme notes

The grandiloquent First Piano Concerto is a work of heroic proportions, which calls for a dynamic performance from the soloist. Liszt himself premièred it in Weimar in 1855, with the charismatic Berlioz as conductor.

George Stubbs 'White horse frightened by a Lion' (detail). The Walker Art Gallery, Liverpool

Piano Concerto no. 1 in E flat major

Liszt leaves no doubt in the score about how he wants the Concerto to open. Over the music he has written *marcato* (emphatic), *deciso* (firmly) and *tempo giusto* (in exact time) and the opening bars are indeed decisive. In complete unison, the strings launch abruptly into an ominous descending figure, short firm bow strokes etching each note sharply on the ear. A strident fanfare on brass and woodwind punctuates the figure like an exclamation mark and the strings repeat the figure even deeper, punctuated by an even more strident fanfare. Clearly Liszt does not intend us to forget these string figures; they are to form the theme (Example 1) that dominates the Concerto.

Oddly enough, when Liszt was asked what his theme meant, he went to the piano and sang the words, 'Das versteht Ihr alle nicht,' as he played the theme. The phrase means, 'This none of you understand,' and of course no one did.

Example 1

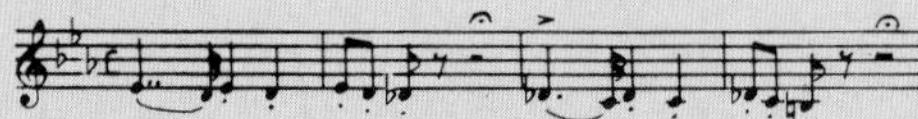

Immediately the theme is over, the piano enters with a resounding thump of a chord, played *fortissimo* (very loud) with the loud pedal down to give the maximum resonance. And a series of octaves – when the pianist plays the same note in four different places at the same time – roll up the keyboard like a shockwave. Another

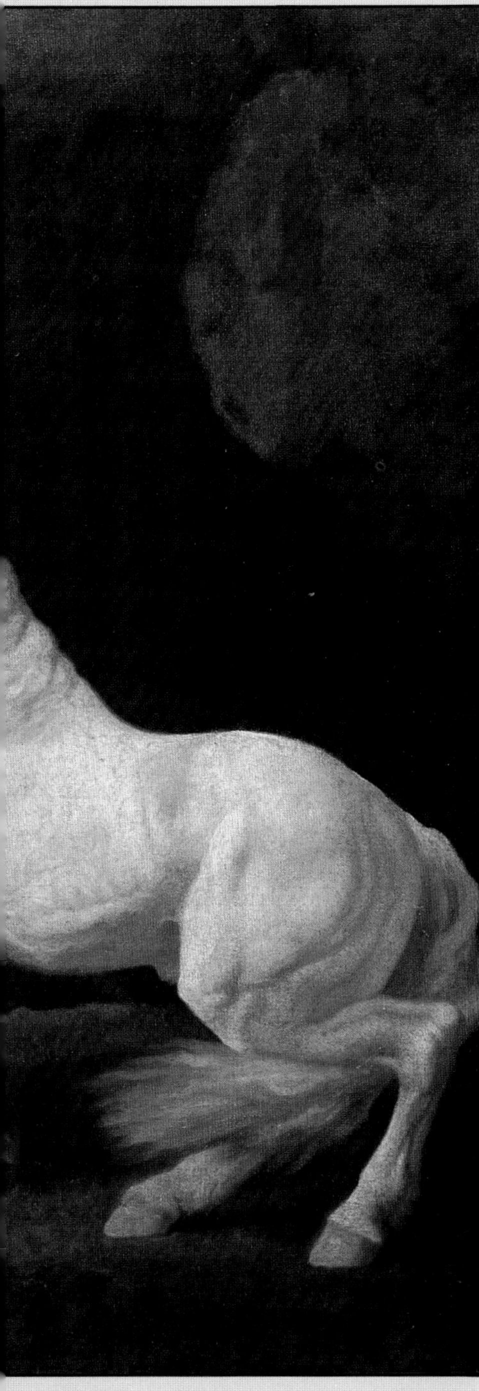

Mauro Pucciarelli

'As a horse to an Arab': so said Liszt about his piano. The image is a potent one, the horse being a Romantic symbol of energy.

Liszt, the 'magician of the keyboard' (above), conjures up a glittering world of fantasy, peopled by lovers and demons.

hammerblow of a chord with similar reverberations and the pianist is off like a conquering hero into a brilliant solo passage.

In few concertos is the piano entry quite so dramatic and it has a reputation among pianists as being notoriously difficult to carry off. But in comparison to the almost unplayable early version, it does not make unreasonable demands. It seems that Liszt must have simplified it to ensure that the pianist achieved the effect he was after.

Towards the end of the solo, a high trill runs into a shower of glittering notes and the mood changes dramatically. A solo clarinet breathes a calming air and ushers in a new melody. The piano passage that follows is one of the most poignantly beautiful that Liszt ever wrote. It seems almost as if, with the tension released, the piano breaks down into impassioned weeping – the pianist is instructed to play *appassionato* while the solo cello which joins in later plays *espressivo*.

But the lyrical mood is soon dispelled. As the strings build up the pace, bassoon and cello hint at the opening theme, before it is reintroduced in a massive *tutti* passage (where all the orchestra play, leaving the piano silent). But the piano soon drives the orchestra to seek shelter, with an incredible flight of descending octaves, sparked off by a barely recognizable variation of the opening theme.

Then, after an extended repeat of the opening piano solo, with strings and bassoon again quietly interjecting the main theme, the first 'movement' draws quietly to a close as if the storm had finally exhausted itself.

Quasi Adagio

The slow passage is marked *Quasi Adagio* because although the main melody is slow and lyrical, it is laid over a rapid pulse that adds intensity and gives the music an underlying edginess even in the calmest moments.

A moody passage on strings ushers in an important new theme, which is to reappear many times. Yet its appearance is rather unsettling here because the descending section could lead anywhere. The uncertainty seems to be resolved, however, when the piano sweeps in and turns the theme into a lovely dreamy melody (Example 2).

Typically, Liszt highlights the melody by allowing the pianist's right hand to play only the notes of the melody, while the left hand underscores it with gentle waves of broken chords.

Example 2

But when the strings return with the theme, they corrupt this innocent, dreamy melody into something sinister, simply by changing the last chord, and playing it loud and *tremolando* (vibrating). The chord is in fact a 'diminished seventh' – ending a phrase with a tremolando diminished seventh was very popular with the Romantics because it injected drama and the feeling that virtually anything could happen. And true to form, the piano launches into a passionate, sensuous sequence. Only when the passion has abated does a solo flute bring a fresh melody to the scene, like a breath of morning air, echoed by gentle breezes on solo clarinet, oboe and then cello, while the piano trills like a chorus of birds.

Scherzando

Then, with a little tinkle on the triangle, pizzicato (plucked) strings lead the orchestra away into a merry dance, the triangle running alongside.

In his review of the first performance of the Concerto, the critic, Eduard Hanslick, ridiculed the use of the triangle and called the work a 'Triangle Concerto': the name has stuck. But Liszt stood firm and retained the triangle in all his later versions, and was moved to defend the use of all kinds of unusual percussion effects – thus anticipating many modern composers.

The merry mood is dampened when the

Understanding music: the symphonic poem

During his years at Weimar, Liszt completed a series of 12 pieces of music which, though not uniformly brilliant, were quite revolutionary in conception. He called these pieces *Symphonische Dichtung*, 'symphonic poems', and they were to have a profound effect on music for the rest of the century.

Of course, the symphonic poem had many precedents. In many ways it is simply another offspring of the burgeoning Romantic preoccupation with meaning in music, expressed particularly in programme music. Later in the century, the distinction between the symphonic poem and programme music became very blurred. Indeed, Liszt's symphonic poems owe a great deal to Berlioz.

But the symphonic poem as Liszt conceived it is not programme music in the sense that Berlioz's *Symphonie Fantastique* is. The extra-musical idea, usually literary, does not dictate the structure of the symphonic poem, except in the very loosest sense; it does not provide a 'programme'. The symphonic poem is essentially a free-form symphony composed to express an idea, whether the idea be literary, historical or just pure fantasy.

Liszt's own symphonic poems were based largely on poems, from *Ce qu'on entend sur la montagne*, based on a poem by the French Romantic novelist Victor Hugo, to *Die Ideale* based on a poem by the German poet Schiller – although *Hunnenschlacht* was inspired by a fresco depicting the battle between Attila's Huns and the Christians defending Rome in 451 AD. But the poems never dictate to the music; they inspire it, or, quite often simply guide the listener to the 'true' meaning of the piece.

Musée des Beaux-Arts de Strasbourg

Liszt's symphonic poem,* Mazeppa *(above), illustrates the dramatic theme of 'mortal man tied to the saddle of genius'.

Later in life, Liszt claimed that during the years at Weimar (1848–61), he had been inspired by the idea of rejuvenating Music 'through an intimate alliance with Poetry; a development more free, and also more expressive, more in keeping with the spirit of the times.'

Whether he rejuvenated music is debatable, but composers all over Europe took up the idea of the symphonic poem enthusiastically – although equally many composers (and critics) rejected it. The composer Smetana, for instance, visited Liszt in Weimar in 1857 and immediately on his return wrote symphonic poems on Shakespeare's *Richard III* (1857–8), Schiller's *Wallenstein's Lager* (1858–9) and the Danish poet Oehlenschläger's *Hakon Jarl* (1861).

But the term itself did not spread rapidly – even Smetana did not call these three works 'symphonic poems' until much later. This is partly because the form is so loose that it is difficult to tell whether a piece is a symphonic poem or not.

In one direction, the symphonic poem became inextricably linked with nationalist movements. Smetana went on to write his famous *Ma Vlast* ('My country') about Czechoslovakia; Dvořák wrote his *Slavonic Dances* and other symphonic poems; and so too did Janáček. In Russia, Balakirev wrote *Tamara* and Borodin wrote *In the Steppes of Central Asia.*

But it is often the shorter, more dramatic pieces which have proved enduringly popular – pieces like Saint-saens' *Danse Macabre,* Dukas' *L'apprenti-sorcier* (The sorcerer's apprentice) and Musorgsky's *St John's Night on the Bare Mountain.*

As the Romantic era drifted towards its end, symphonic poems – if indeed they can be called that – became more and more impressionistic. Debussy referred to his *Prélude à l'après-midi d'un Faune* (1892–4) for a Mallarmé poem as a 'very free illustration'. But even this illustrative idea soon fell out of favour in the light of 20th century realism, and after 1920, fewer symphonic poems were written.

piano moodily plays the main theme again (Example 1). Rising strings build the pace and drama up to a mighty restatement of the theme on trombones, followed by the piano's hammer chord from the opening of the Concerto. The fresh morning flute theme from the *Adagio* breaks in but is soon engulfed as the music rises to another climax – this time, it is a rapid bugle blast from the trumpets that provides the impetus.

In contrast to the dynamic First Concerto, the Second Concerto is much more lyrical and romantic in character. It has the haunting quality of a starry night, though the dreamy mood sometimes borders on the sinister (left).

John Martin 'Arthur and Aegle' (detail). Laing Art Gallery/Tyne & Wear County Council Museums

Allegro marziale animato

The final movement opens with a startling transformation of the *Adagio* theme (Example 2). Instead of the dreamy nocturne, it appears as a jolly, if rapid, march, sounding almost like a military band – *marziale* means martial – complete with piccolos and clashing cymbals.

But the trombones grimly intervene, finishing off the theme the march had left incomplete, and the piano launches into its most spectacular sequence yet. The pianist takes earlier themes and transforms them until they are barely recognizable – to create a series of glittering passages.

Then as the march reappears, even faster this time, the music, accompanied by massive octave runs on the piano and a rhythmic repeat of a fragment from the main theme, builds to a spectacular climax.

Piano Concerto no. 2 in A major

In contrast to the heroic E flat major Concerto, the A major Concerto has a lyrical and poetic feel. It opens, not with a dramatic fanfare, but in a dreamy romantic vein, with a quiet, haunting melody on woodwind, the lead moving mercurially from clarinet to oboe and back, to clarinet. A low key entry, perhaps, but the theme introduced is to play an important role.

Example 3

Unusually, the piano enters almost unnoticed, stealing on to the scene with a series of gentle *arpeggios* (a harplike effect in which the pianist runs up through each note of a chord) that spin a dreamy web around the orchestra.

The dreamy mood slips quietly to an end with a deep wistful sigh – an effect created by a piano arpeggio that runs up one note short of the top A like an intake of breath, and allows the strings to finish off with a sigh to the lower A.

Immediately, the piano angrily transforms the theme. But this burst of frustration is soon quelled and the dreamy mood sets in once more. This time, though, the reedy tone of the oboe gives a slightly sinister edge – and the sense that the mood may change dramatically.

A solo horn enters *träumend* (dreaming), followed by solo oboe then cello, while the piano remains accompanist – typical of Liszt's extensive use of solo instruments – to create an effect like orchestral chamber music. But as the emotional intensity threatens to overwhelm, the piano breaks in with a cascade of chords, running in to its first cadenza.

Now the mood changes dramatically as the piano rumbles right down into its deepest register, an area Liszt seemed very fond of. Then with growling, slashing bass chords, it introduces a grim new theme with a powerful *ostinato* (rhythmic) beat.

Example 4

Then, as the piano seems to swell with pride, it bounds off into an accelerating

Ruben's painting, inspired by Mantegna's* Triumph of Caesar, *has the same brash, triumphal character as the final section of Liszt's Second Piano Concerto. Some commentators found this* Marziale *section vulgar, but, well interpreted, it can be magnificent.

Peter Paul Rubens 'A Roman Triumph'/reproduced by courtesy of the Trustees, The National Gallery, London/Chris Barker

chase, *allegro agitato*. A tumbling piano run leads into a strident *tutti* (full orchestral passage) dominated by loud trombone blasts. The hunt is really on. But after a fierce exchange between piano and strings, *fortissimo e violente*, the piano takes the strings into a gentle new melody with the three chords from the opening theme (Example 3).

A soothing cello reworking of this theme in a broader, fuller tempo leads back into a slow, contemplative section. A piano cadenza again proves to be the cue for a change of mood and the ostinato theme (Example 4) reappears in a strutting *allegro deciso* passage. After an exciting, swirling exchange between piano and orchestra, there is a massive climax capped by an avalanche of octaves on the piano.

Immediately, the full orchestra bursts in with a stirring, martial variation of the ostinato theme (Example 4). Many commentators have found this *Marziale* section lacking in taste and indeed, it is less than subtle. But Liszt always believed in making things absolutely clear to his audience in pieces designed for public presentation, and the brash, triumphal sound does provide an effective contrast with the rest of the Concerto. It seems to be the finale, but just as it reaches the climax, aided by bell-like trills on the piano, the piano breaks off into its reflective dreamy mood once more.

Earlier themes are transformed and run together by piano and solo instruments, before the pace and drama build to a powerful climax. Then with spectacular *glissandos* (where the pianist runs a finger rapidly down the keyboard), the Concerto is brought to a triumphant close.

Waring Abbott/Phonogram International

André Previn, the conductor (above).

Great interpreters

Misha Dichter (pianist)

Dichter is one of the newer generation of concert pianists born after World War Two. He is American, coming from a Polish family background. He leapt to prominence in the international arena when he won Second Prize in the Third International Tchaikovsky Piano Competition in Moscow at the age of 21. He made his US début later that year, 1966, and in 1967 with the New Philharmonia in London. Since then he has toured incessantly, consolidating his position as a fine interpreter, especially of the romantic keyboard repertoire.

André Previn (conductor)

Born in Berlin in 1929, André Previn migrated with his family to Los Angeles in 1939. He studied piano and composition from a very early age and by the late 40s was working as a professional jazz pianist and orchestrator in Hollywood. In 1949 he completed his first original film score for MGM, *The Sun Comes Up*. While his career in the jazz and film world was marked by continuing success, he began in the 50s to study for a career as a concert pianist and conductor. This eventually led to his conducting début, in 1963, with the St Louis Symphony Orchestra: the same year he won his fourth Oscar for a film score since 1959.

His first conducting appointment was with the Houston Symphony Orchestra, a position held from 1967–70. In 1965 he began, through records, his long association with the London Symphony

Orchestra which led to him becoming principal conductor from 1969 to 1979. During this period his appearances in many guises and situations, both on television and in concerts round the world, gave him a very considerable reputation both with the critics and the music loving public. He has now become one of the most famous and popular figures associated with classical music in the world today, appearing as guest conductor or performer with virtually every famous orchestra. He has been principal conductor of the Pittsburgh Symphony Orchestra since 1976.

Previn is entirely at home with the big romantic works of the last century, and leads the Pittsburgh Symphony with the right amount of fire and clarity to propel the soloist to inspired heights.

FURTHER LISTENING

Hungarian Rhapsodies, G 359
Liszt was an avid collector of melodies and songs from all sources, and it is not surprising to find that he transcribed nearly 20 Hungarian folk and gypsy tunes for piano. In doing so, he transformed them into something wholly personal in flavour and expression. Later in life he orchestrated six of the original piano pieces, and these have remained amongst his most popular works. Full of life and colour these open-natured pieces have an immediacy which will always guarantee their popularity.

Sonata in B Minor, G 178 (1853)
As is appropriate with one of the world's greatest piano virtuosos, Liszt's reputation lies mainly with his solo keyboard compositions. With the B Minor Sonata we come across a true masterpiece. The work's form revolves around endless, inspired variations upon four short themes, an idea the composer borrowed from Schubert's *Wanderer Fantasy*. Within this compass, Liszt succeeds in building up an entire world of music and feeling.

Rigoletto Paraphrase, G 434 (1859)
Liszt constantly needed an input of small concert pieces for his life as a performing artist, and his natural appreciation of works by his contemporaries often led him to transcribe pieces by composers such as Beethoven, Wagner and Verdi. These works demonstrate a phenomenal piano conception and technique, rendering as they do whole orchestral scores into charming arrangements for just one pianist. The Rigoletto Paraphrase from Verdi's famous opera is a fine example of this.

IN THE BACKGROUND

'Like men possessed'

Lionized by society, hero-worshipped by audiences, the virtuosos were the superstars of the age. Through their extraordinary technical brilliance they exalted music into new realms of popularity.

With his powerful hands and sunken, distorted face – the result of successive jawbone operations – it is easy to see how Paganini's (left) uncanny virtuosity was often perceived as diabolic. This legand echoed the career of the great Tartini (d.1770) an 18th century virtuoso violinist. Tartini (right) wrote his famous Devil's Sonata *after a dream in which the devil had played the violin with 'consummate skill'.*

BBC Hulton Picture Library

When Niccolò Paganini played the violin, people said they could see the devil standing at his elbow; when Franz Liszt stormed up and down the keyboard, the audience went hysterical. Between them these two great virtuosos inspired, hypnotized, entranced and awed a whole generation. Yet towering though Paganini and Liszt were, they were not the only virtuosos to set aflame the hearts of contemporary audiences, nor yet necessarily the most technically accomplished.

The fervid imagination of the romantics, which seemed to embrace the rising middle class, demanded heroes. Pianists should not simply be accomplished musicians, but knights of the keyboard. And pianists from all over Europe seemed to spring up to meet this demand. There was Liszt's great rival, Sigismond Thalberg, who people swore must have three hands; there was the Bohemian titan Alexander Dreyshock with his startling octaves; Alkan the recluse; de Meyer the clown, who played with his elbows; the Viennese dandy who took America by storm, Henri Herz; Louis Gottschalk; and many others, not to mention the great composer pianists such as Mendelssohn and Chopin.

There had of course been virtuosos before, from Vivaldi to Mozart, but never had they been in the public eye in such a way before. In the days when serious music was the reserve of the wealthy patrons, the virtuoso was appreciated by just a handful of connoisseurs. As the middle class grew, however, and patronage began to decline, music was forced to reach an ever widening audience – indeed, anyone with the price of a concert ticket in their pocket.

What this new audience demanded more than anything was pianists. During the early decades of the 19th century, the piano had found its way into nearly every well-to-do household in Europe. it was not just a musical instrument; it was an integral part of social life. Few soirées would be complete without a musical interlude around the piano. Like fine needlework and light conversation, playing the piano – or singing to it – was an essential social accomplishment for any young lady of good breeding. Naturally, it was pianists people wanted to see, and pianists are what they got.

From 1815 onwards pianists began to travel all over Europe, and sometimes beyond, playing cities and towns, big halls and small. Not only were there many pianists, but the popularity of the piano as well had opened the way for many talented players. New conservatoires, founded in Paris (1795) and London (1822) for example, were turning out a score of graduates a year all relying more and more on public concerts to earn a living.

As the audience constantly demanded fresh excitement, in the form of new players, it was no good a pianist staying in one place – audiences would soon decline. It was essential to keep on the move.

Liszt (right) was so impressed by Paganini performances with the violin that he resolved to do the same for the piano. Like his virtuoso mentor, he acquired a demonic reputation, although he was also likened to a god. Playing like a man possessed, Liszt also 'possessed' his audiences, especially their female members, with his electrifying showmanship.

James Marshall 'Tartini's Dream'. Schackgalerie, Munich/Joachim Blauel/Artothek

Nationalgalerie, Staatliche Museen Preussischer Kulturbesitz

Although many gravitated to Paris, which was blessed by a phenomenal wealth of pianistic talent and remarkably appreciative audiences, few stayed for long periods. Even the frail Chopin undertook a punishing tour of England and Scotland. The age of the touring virtuoso had begun.

The touring virtuoso

Touring was by no means easy. The railway network was not established until the 1840s, and travel was slow and exhausting, especially in winter. Few concert halls existed, and there was little in the way of management and organization to run the business side of the concert circuit, from booking halls and musicians to printing programmes and arranging accommodation for the soloist. Even in Paris, François Habeneck did not establish the *Société des Concerts du Conservatoire* until 1828. Advance notice of the event would often be nothing more than the gossip of travellers arriving slightly ahead of the performer. The travel-worn virtuoso would probably have to perform, without rehearsal, on an indifferent instrument – with even more indifferent musicians, hurriedly assembled for the performance. Ignaz Moscheles, for instance, an older contemporary of Liszt's, found himself in Liverpool in 1825 with eight strings and 'four halting wind instruments' for his concerto accompaniment. Yet Moscheles was at that time a major virtuoso, on a par with Kalkbrenner and Hummel. He lived long enough, until 1870, to become an anachronism, but in 1825 his star was high. Although he had started off as a bravura pianist, by this time he was a dedicated 'pure' musician, the first touring virtuoso to try to bring Beethoven and other quality music to the public and a major figure in the transition to the high Romantic virtuoso – someone who could perform the best music on offer.

The kind of touring schedule the virtuosos undertook would be considered demanding even with today's organization and transport. The violinist Paganini, for instance, played 112 concerts in less than a year when he toured the British Isles between the spring of 1831 and 1832. As there was little time for rehearsal, pianists would naturally tend to choose a few favourite pieces. In 1818, the pianist Johann Tomaschek wrote:

Never settled in one place, always touring, always busy preparing programmes for concerts, they never have time to study anything new. As a result, most of their programmes are mostly repetitions of earlier programmes, except that pieces may be presented in a different order.

Up until 1830, touring was intense, but fairly low key. Then, however, two events changed the picture. First, there was the gradual fanning of the Romantic flame right across Europe. People began to expect more of the virtuoso. He took on more and more the aura of the hero, the warrior, the great Artist – in Schumann's words 'a daring fellow, whose fate is to conquer and rule, not with the dangerous tools of combat, but with the peaceful tools of art'. They looked to be thrilled and inspired by the skill and passion of the virtuosos. People began to go to virtuoso concerts not simply to listen to great playing, but to be enthralled, amazed, overcome.

Paganini

Second, and not entirely disconnected, there was Paganini. Paganini had long been recognized in his

Whereas the 18th-century orchestra had to contend with audiences (right) that chatted, ate, drank and flirted throughout performances, the rise of the great virtuosos was accompanied by a rise in the status of musicians and a correspondingly respectful audience.

Before the arrival of instrumental virtuosos in the late 18th century, the soprano singing voices of castrati (male singers who were castrated around the age of seven) enjoyed the greatest adulation. Among the most famous of these castrato singers was Farinelli (below). The last known castrato died in 1922.

Royal College of Music

native Italy as a talented violinist, but when, at the a of 45, he began to tour Europe in 1828, the effect w cataclysmic. During the next four years, Pagani played in all the major cities of western Europe, ar his tour was more than just a tour, it was a triumph progress that left everyone, musicians and publi awestruck in its wake.

Technically, Paganini was undoubtedly brillian combining many different strands of virtuosity in way no one had done before. He played scale passag and arpeggios at breakneck speed – Michelange Abbado observed that he played his *Sonata mouvement perpetuel* at an incredible tempo of 1 notes a second at his Paris concert in 1832. He ma phenomenal use of harmonics, pizzicato, bow tric and lefthand plucking – in his variations on *God Sa the Queen,* he would play the melody complete wi double stops with the bow, while plucking the ba line with his left hand! And his speciality was melodi played on the G-string alone.

Even this was not crucial, however, other virtuo violinists could perform equally dazzling feats, thoug few could perform quite as many. What was cruci was the effect Paganini had on his audience.

When he began touring, Paganini, by then in his mi 40s, was a spectral, riveting figure. Suffering fro syphilis and other health problems, he had had all h teeth removed shortly before his appearance in Pari And his dishevelled hair hung in two lank locks either side of his pallid, hollow face, while one gau shoulder sat higher than the other. His very uglines combined with his intense personality and the da eyes that blazed hypnotically from their deep socke gave him a magnetic, demonic quality that few cou ever forget. Few people could see him without feelin that there was something a little frightening abo him. Berlioz describes his first meeting with him, aft a performance of the *Symphonie Fantastique* December 1833:

Liszt caricatured as a superstar (left). His besotted lady fans provided forms of audience participation – clapping, fainting, ogling and showering him with flowers – that contrasted dramatically with the haughty lack of interest of earlier audiences.

. . a man waited for me alone in the hall, a man with ong hair, a keen eye, a strange and ravaged face – a ossessed genius, a colossus among giants, whom I ad never seen, and the first glimpse of whom isturbed me deeply . . . it was Paganini!!

Even the sober Charles Hallé describes the 'striking, we-inspiring, ghost-like figure of Paganini' and how e sat spellbound, 'a shudder running through me henever his uncanny eyes fell upon me'.

When Paganini took to the stage in his black tailcoat nd began to play, the effect was hypnotic – few could ter give a dispassionate account of his performance. ll were carried away by the frenzied intensity of his laying. People talk of the supernatural, dreamlike uality, how they felt – very little about the erformance. Even the critic of the serious *Leipziger lusikalische Zeitung* was moved to talk about 'a orld we may have experienced before, but only in reams', and about a 'hidden cloven hoof'.

No wonder people began to talk about pacts with ne devil and how some even believed they could see ne devil at his elbow guiding his arm. He seemed to be ne very epitome of Faust, who was then becoming a ult figure through the influence of Goethe's drama nd Christopher Marlowe's play. Faust is the conjuror ho is persuaded by the devil's agent Mephistopheles) sell his soul to the devil in exchange for power and nowledge. The idea of this devilish talent and the lost oul had tremendous fascination for the Romantics – iszt himself wrote many pieces on the theme. And aganini seemed to be Faust, Mephistopheles and the evil all rolled into one.

Of course, for a long while, Paganini did little to ispel these fancies – even the rumours that suggested e had murdered his mistress (or her lover) and that e now used her intestine for his fourth string. It was aluable publicity. And it is in this that Paganini's nfluence lay. It showed the great advantages of publicity, how personality was as important as technical skill for the virtuoso, and, above all, the importance of putting on a show. It is no coincidence that Paganini inspired a merchandizing operation comparable in its scope to some of those of the 20th century – people flocked to buy hats, dresses, perfumes, gloves and walking sticks *à la* Paganini.

In the days before recording technology, concert tours (and teaching) were a vital source of income for virtuosos. But poor roads, bad publicity, inadequate instruments and unrehearsed accompanists were regular occupational hazards between venues such as Rome (below) and Paris.

Mauro Pucciarelli

Thalberg

When people went to a concert, they expected to see a show, to be excited, or to see a great personality; they rarely went just for the music. Some virtuosos, like the high-minded Clara Schumann, insisted on

Ignaz Moscheles (below) brought a crisp and incisive touch to his own piano-playing, but he found the effects of some other virtuosos, notably Chopin, too showy.

Bildarchiv Preussischer Kulturbesitz

Archiv für Kunst und Geschichte

Dreyshock's (above) virtuosic speciality was octaves. When he played in Munich it was said that his octaves – which needed 16 hours of practice a day – could be heard in Paris.

giving serious music concerts without a hint of showmanship, but most others not merely succumbed but positively revelled in the 'showbiz' possibilities of the piano virtuoso.

Flamboyance was the order of the day, and each virtuoso struggled to outdo the next in the extravagance of their effects. Rivalry was not merely fierce, but cultivated – it was useful publicity. Audiences loved to think of the idea of two or even more titans of the keyboard battling it out. While Henri Herz was touring the United States at the same time as Leopold de Meyer, they conducted a protracted battle in the columns of local newspapers in long letters addressed 'To the Public'. The incident that provoked it – de Meyer's pianos were left in the concert hall that Herz was due to play in – was remarkably trivial, but they both made the most of the controversy, which the American public thoroughly enjoyed.

One of the more popular events was a showdown between two – or more – colossi of the piano. Of these by far the most eagerly awaited was the battle between Sigismond Thalberg and Liszt.

Thalberg was a completely different character from Liszt and he cultivated the idea of achieving the most spectacular of pianistic effects with the minimum of visible effort. He would sit at the piano virtually motionless while dazzling audiences with a technique that seemed to rival Liszt's. His speciality was a sequence that sounded as if it could not possibly be played with less than three hands – every virtuoso had to have a trick like this. Thalberg's was achieved by playing the melody with his thumbs while accompanying it with arpeggios, both above and below. It was this that gave him his nickname 'Old Arpeggio'.

Of Thalberg's playing, Mendelssohn, who was quite a pianist himself, wrote that it was:

an accumulation of the finest and most exquisite effects, a crescendo of difficulties and embellishments that is astonishing. Everything is so calculated and so polished, and shows such assurance, skill and superlative effects . . . he is unique.

However, Mendelssohn's use of the word 'calculated' is significant – for that indeed is what his approach to music seemed to be. It seems that despite his dazzling technique, he was lacking in poetry. Chopin wrote a succinct and clever summary of Thalberg in 1830:

As for Thalberg, he plays excellently, but he is not my man. Younger than I, pleases the ladies, makes pot pourries from La Muette *[an opera by Auber], gets his soft passages by the pedal, not the hand, takes tenths as easily as I take octaves – has diamond shirt studs – does not admire Moscheles.*

Nevertheless, for a while, Thalberg seriously rivalled Liszt, and while Liszt was away from Paris with Countess Marie d'Agoult, Thalberg was denting his crown. On his return, Liszt was spoiling for a fight. After writing a scathing review in the *Gazette Musicale,* Liszt wrote to George Sand that he had wanted to make a study of Thalberg's complete works, 'so I shut myself in for a whole afternoon to study them conscientiously'. Thalberg could be equally cutting. There is a story that Liszt suggested a two-handed concert, to which Thalberg replied, 'No . . . I do not like to be accompanied.'

Finally, the eccentric Princess Belgiojoso managed to arrange a play-off between the two giants in her salon on 31 March, 1837. Everyone who was anyone in Paris was there. It was quite an affair. Not only were Liszt and Thalberg there to fight it out – so too were Chopin, Herz, Czerny (Beethoven's pupil and Liszt's teacher) and Pixis, all major virtuosos. When it came to the crunch, Thalberg played brilliantly and dazzled his audience – but there was no contest; Liszt was king.

Spectacular events like this were the order of the day. When Henri Herz made his first performance in England on 2 July 1838, he performed, with other musicians, Czerny's *Concertstücke,* arranged for no fewer than 8 pianos and 12 harps.

The showmen

Henri Herz was an elegant pianist but an out and out showman with no pretence. He was probably out to make money – and this is just what he did. Herz had a beautiful house in Paris, earned four times as much as any other virtuoso, set up his own piano-makers and built a concert hall. He probably toured more than any other virtuoso, and when he went to the United States, not untypically, he used a press agent called Bernard Ullman who once said to Herz:

I will take care of the announcements of your concerts. I will have your programs printed, I will see to it that everything is in order in the hall where you will give the concert, I will bring you to the attention of the newspapers. The papers are the nerves of artistic success, just as money is the nerves of war.

And this is just what Ullman did, organizing ever more spectacular publicity for Herz. One of Ullman's ideas was a concert lighted by 1000 candles, which greatly delighted the public and was an instant success. Another was for a massive event with speeches, giant choirs and a Grand March arranged for 40 pianos – all on an American nationalist theme. In the end, Herz just played the March with 8 pianos, but

BBC Hulton Picture Library

Sigismond Thalberg's audiences craned their necks to view his celebrated 'three-handed' effects at the keyboard. Unlike Paginini, however, Thalberg (left) was a polished aristocrat with a smooth and dignified demeanour.

Finale furioso

BBC Hulton Picture Library

This caricature of a virtuoso in action (above) illustrates how the star pianist enslaved his audience with displays of pianistic 'fireworks'. Indeed, the great virtuosos were sometimes revered more for their agility and versatility as performers in the widest sense of the work, than for the quality of the music produced.

the event was also a success. The age of publicity and showmanship was here to stay.

Another man out to dazzle – if not deafen – the audience but perhaps little else was Alexander Dreyshock. He must have been quite a pianist, for when he arrived in Paris in 1843, a reviewer began to talk about a new trinity of piano virtuosos with Liszt the Father, Thalberg the son and Dreyshock the Holy Ghost. But Dreyshock was anything but ghostly – his playing was reckoned loud enough to wake the dead. Heine suggested that people in Paris could hear him playing in Munich if the wind was right. He was to Heine a 'god of thunder' whose octave playing was truly spectacular – he was apparently able to play Chopin's *Revolutionary* Etude replacing the left-hand passages – with octaves – an impressive feat.

Dreyshock, like many other virtuosos on the circuit, was giving the public what they wanted. Even Liszt, who could really play poetically when he wanted to, regarded himself as a servant of the public and would give the public what they wanted – bravura display, fantasies on popular operatic themes and pot-pourris of familiar tunes.

Liszt, like so many virtuosos, relied on the strength of his personality to make his impression on the audience. This was not only showmanship, it was musically important as well. As Schumann says, 'If Liszt were to play behind the scenes, a considerable part of the poetry would be lost.'

Liszt himself, like Paganini, deliberately cultivated the Mephistophelian mystery he seemed to possess – it was an important part of his effect. All the major virtuosos seemed to throw themselves at the piano, trying to work themselves and the audience into a frenzy of passion. The hysteria of the audience and the intensity of their performance must have sometimes taken them over so that for a few moments they played, as they fantasized, 'like men possessed'.

Liszt's influence on the succeeding generation of pianists was enormous. Indeed, every budding virtuoso in Europe wanted to come and learn his craft at the Master's classes in Weimar – among them the brilliant Carl Tausig, reckoned by some to be the most complete virtuoso of all time. Another was a young Russian who looked like a reincarnation of Beethoven, Anton Rubinstein. Rubinstein as a boy emulated Liszt's dynamic, showy style and travelled to see Liszt in 1846 and enrol as a pupil. But for some reason, the perenially generous Liszt told him to 'win the goal of his ambition by his own unassisted efforts'. And that is precisely what Rubinstein did in a way perhaps never contemplated by Liszt – the greatest virtuoso of the them all.

Anton Rubinstein (below) was the first great European virtuoso to tour America. Rubinstein's 'Historical Recitals' covering the entire development of keyboard music were legendary.

BBC Hulton Picture Library

Contemporary composers

Vincenzo Bellini (1801-35)

Born in Catania, Sicily, he was taught at first by his musical grandfather before being sent to the Naples Conservatory in 1819, where he remained for six years. His first work to attract notice was the opera *Bianca e Fernando,* produced in 1826, quickly followed by *Il Pirata,* first produced in Milan in 1827. Its success made him famous throughout Europe. Further operas, embodying the Italian operatic tradition's *bel canto* style, followed: *La Straniera, I Capuleti ed i Montecchi, Norma,* often written with Romani as his librettist. In 1835 he travelled to Paris, where *I Puritani di Scozia* was a huge success. His death, from an intestinal complaint, was sudden and unexpected. He was admired by Wagner, Schumann, Berlioz and Tchaikovsky.

Muzio Clementi (1752-1832)

Born in Rome, Clementi was organist at a minor church in 1766 when he was discovered by a wealthy Englishman, Peter Beckford (cousin of the writer William Beckford), and taken to England to be his 'pianist in residence'. In 1779 Clementi published his first six piano sonatas as Opus 2, which established his reputation by their brilliance. In 1780 he toured Europe, playing before Queen Marie Antoinette of France and competing with Mozart in Vienna. Mozart admired his techniques if not his compositions. Back in London, Clementi published 60 piano sonatas, some later admired by Beethoven, before being eclipsed by Haydn on his London visits. Clementi, however, continued to teach, founded a publishing company, which published Beethoven's works later, invested in piano manufacturing and became very rich. His *Gradus ad Parnassum* was very well-known. After making a final visit to the Continent, Clementi died in England.

Gaetano Donizetti (1797-1848)

Born in Bergamo, northern Italy, he studied with Padrei Matei in Bologna. His first opera was produced in Venice in 1818, but his first real success came with *Zoraide di Granata,* first performed in Rome in 1822. This led to a contract with the Neapolitan theatres and international fame in 1830 with *Anna Bolena,* produced in Milan. In the next decade Donizetti had huge success with operas like *Lucrezia Borgia, Marina Faliero* and *Lucia di Lammermoor,* all showing Rossini's influence. Further fame came in 1843 with *Don Pasquale* in Paris, but by that time Donizetti was severely ill with syphilis and in 1844 he was confined to a lunatic asylum, where he died.

John Field (1782-1837)

Born in Dublin, Field was a prodigy by the age of 10, becoming a pupil of Clementi in London and winning Haydn's praise. He performed his First Piano Concerto in 1799 and then set off with Clementi on a European tour. Refusing instruction by Beethoven's teacher, Albrechtsberger, in Vienna, Field travelled on to Russia, where he found his spiritual home and where he was to die. By 1812 he published his first three pieces called *Nocturne,* which dispense with string accompaniment and have a sustained melody and lyrical harmony that anticipate Chopin. During the next 10 years he composed most of his major works – more nocturnes, another sonata and some chamber music with piano. By 1821 he had acquired a nearly legendary reputation throughout Europe. Field died in Russia in 1837.

Niccolo Paganini (1782-1840)

Born to a poor family in Genoa, Italy, Paganini was taught the elements of violin playing by his father, and soon became a virtuoso performer. After studying with Alessandro Rolla, he went on his first concert tour of northern Italy at the age of 15. After his Milan recital in 1813, Paganini lived as a travelling virtuoso, spending much time in northern Europe. In 1831 he gave 59 concerts within six months in Britain. His fantastic appearance and technique made him a 'star'. Notorious for his gambling and womanizing, he made and lost fortunes, and died almost bankrupt killed by varied venerial and pulmonary diseases. He rarely played the music of others, writing his own to display his own powers. But his *Capricci,* published in 1820, were transcribed by Liszt, Schumann and Brahms for their haunting quality. He vastly extended violin techniques, using the upper reaches of the instrument freely, and was a master of personal publicity.

Bibliography

G. Abraham, *Chopin's Musical Style,* Greenwood Press, Westport, 1980

M. Brown, *Schubert: A Critical Biography,* Da Capo, New York, 1977

M. Brown, *Schubert Symphonies,* University of Washington Press, Seattle, 1971

R. Cappell, *Schubert's Songs,* Da Capo, New York, 1977

J. Eigelberger, *Schubert as Seen by his Pupils,* Cambridge Univerity Press, Cambridge, 1986

A. Einstein, *Schubert,* Panther, London, 1971

B. Ferra, *Chopin and George Sand in Majorca,* Haskell, New York, 1974

A. Hedley, *Chopin,* Littlefield, Totowa, 1977

A. Hutchings, *Schubert,* Littlefield, Totowa, 1977

G. Marek and M. Gordon-Smith, *Chopin,* Harper and Row, New York, 1978

G. Marek, *Schubert: A Biography,* Viking Press, New York, 1985

D. Melville, *Chopin: A Biography,* Shoestring Press, Hamden, 1977

J. Methuen-Campbell, *Chopin-playing from the Composer to the Present Day,* Taplinger, New York, 1981

A. Orga, *Chopin: His Life and Times,* Hippocrene Books, New York, 1978

C. Osborne, *Schubert and His Vienna,* Knopf, New York, 1985

C. Rostand, *Liszt,* Marion Boyars Publishers, London, 1980

J. Reed, *Schubert Song Companion,* Universe, New York, 1985

S. Sitwell, *Liszt,* Dover, London, 1968

A. Walker, *Franz Liszt: The Virtuoso Years, 1811-47,* Faber and Faber, London, 1983

D. Watson, *Liszt,* J. M. Dent, London, 1983

H. Weinstock, *Chopin: The Man and His Music,* Da Capo, New York, 1983

H. Westerley, *Liszt: The Composer and His Piano Works,* Longwood Publishing Group, Dover, 1977

Index

Note Page numbers in italic refer to illustrations.